From a DRUNKARD To a Pastor
Discovering Completeness In Christ

Jim Moreland

WESTBOW
PRESS®
A DIVISION OF THOMAS NELSON
& ZONDERVAN

Scripture taken from the New King James Version®. Copyright © 1982
by Thomas Nelson. Used by permission. All rights reserved.

WestBow Press books may be ordered through booksellers or by contacting:

WestBow Press
A Division of Thomas Nelson & Zondervan
1663 Liberty Drive
Bloomington, IN 47403
www.westbowpress.com
1 (866) 928-1240

ISBN: 978-1-9736-5754-5 (sc)
ISBN: 978-1-9736-5753-8 (hc)
ISBN: 978-1-9736-5755-2 (e)

Library of Congress Control Number: 2019903226

Print information available on the last page.

WestBow Press rev. date: 04/22/2019

Contents

Dedication

I am dedicating this book to the prayer warriors in my family that never gave up praying for me. First, I want to recognize my mom, who always saw the good in me when there was not any good to see. My sisters Dixie, Mary and Nancy, who were Christians long before I joined God's family and I believe their prayers, had a lot to do with praying me into the family of God. Finally, My Aunt Maxine, who has been a Christian as far back as I can remember and has been a real inspiration to me. I am so blessed to have all them in my earthly family and someday I am looking forward to all of us being together in heaven.

Introduction

As exciting as it was for me to write the *Rising from Ashes* book (A Christ-centered smoking cessation program). In that book I shared a miraculous deliverance from nicotine addiction. After years of being addicted to nicotine, and harboring feelings of hopelessness I would ever be able to quit smoking; Christ delivered me from that deadly habit. After a few months of reflection on the RFA book, my heart churned inside of me as I recalled all the times God intervened on my behalf. The deliverance I experienced from nicotine addiction was just a small part of all God has done for me through the years. While experiencing such an eye-opening revelation, and finally realizing my nearsightedness. Feelings of remorse saddened me for not giving God credit for the many times he has touched my life and kept me from harm. That is the inspiration for writing this second book, and to give God his well-deserved glory. And to proclaim, to all, that you can never be so lost in your addictions or sinful behavior that God cannot reach down from heaven and pluck you from that nightmare. God is a master life-restorer; let him restore yours.

In the pages of this book, I share my salvation story from the darkest of times to when Jesus brought me into his glorious light and began to navigate me onto a new and brighter path. The first fifty years of my life was a time of overwhelming fear, pain, brokenness, sorrow, addiction, and shattered relationships. My rebellious existence was fueled by rage, selfishness, and my complete hatred of God. But God never forgot the little boy who humbly sought his forgiveness, while squirming nervously in a small Baptist church.

Speaking extensively about spiritual maturity in the *Rising from ashes* book*,* in this book, I not only want to share my personal testimony, but I also want to explore the steps necessary to reach that sought after spiritual maturity. And how to develop those areas of our lives in which we need to strive to be complete, lacking nothing: spiritually mature. It is not so much the reaching of spiritual maturity that transforms us, but it is the continual striving to reach that completeness that is paramount in our spiritual growth. We may never reach Christ-like perfection in these fleshly bodies, but we must keep trying. We must never give up, no matter the struggles we encounter. Perseverance is a necessary trait to reach our final destination—to be like Jesus.

Being quite honest with you, the more I strive to be like Jesus the more I realize how improbable that is going to be as long as I inhabit this corruptible earthly body. Even though we may never reach complete Christ-likeness while on earth; we must keep striving to reach that goal until the day of Christ's return. When we will shed these corruptible bodies, and appear in our glorious incorruptible spiritual bodies. Then we will truly realize completeness--for we will be like him (Jesus).

After giving my life to Christ in February of 2000, I arrived at the all-encompassing conclusion that before Christ became part of my life I existed in a state of illusion: existing under the false assumption that I was in control of my destiny. Like the sharp pain of a punch in the mouth, I awoke to this truth: humans are in control of very little when it comes to the circumstances of their life. We do not choose our parents, our gender, when or where we will be born, the color of our hair, color of our eyes, or our physical appearance. God controls all of those traits along with all the circumstances of our lives. Scripture teaches that God formed each individual in the confines of their mother's womb, "For you formed my inward parts;

You covered me in my mother's womb. Your eyes saw my substance, being yet unformed" (Psalm 139: 13, 16a).

God gave and controls the very breathe that sustains human life (cf. Genesis 2: 7). God has control over the number of days we have on earth; and each day given is precious in his eyes. It is our obligation to make the best of each one of those days, by resisting the sinful desires of the flesh and; instead, walking in the Spirit of God, "When your days are fulfilled and you rest with your fathers, I will set up your seed after you, who will come from your body, and I will establish his kingdom" (2 Samuel 7:12). Time is life's most precious commodity and time spent with family, friends, and serving Jesus is time's greatest reward--so do not waste time. Time is an exquisite gift and once used up you can never get it back! One of my greatest regrets is wasting fifty years of my life before surrendering my will to Jesus' will.

God's providence covers our children, their children, and the generations that follow. God, if he chooses, can even prolong the days we have on earth, "The fear of the LORD *is* the beginning of wisdom, and the knowledge of the Holy One *is* understanding, For by me your days will be multiplied, and years of life will be added to you" (Proverbs 9:10, 11, italics theirs).

The one thing we are in control of is the choices we make. We can choose to live a life that honors God or we can choose a life that does not honor God. Early in my life I made some really bad decisions, and drinking was only one of those poor decisions. I grew so angry over what I believed were injustices I suffered. I rebelled against God. Because of my anger, I only focused on the past, which blinded me to the wonderful future God wanted to give me. I sprinted as far and as fast from God as I possibly could. But God ran faster than I did, and through his grace, caught me and redeemed me. There was a time when I thought I had all the answers about life, happiness, and the reasons we are here on this earth. Only to discover, I had no right answers at all. I was the lost, of the lost. Are you running from God? If you are, maybe it is time to stop running and turn around. Because he is right on you tail.

Christians are called to Completeness

As followers of Jesus Christ, we are called to completeness, "But let patience have its perfect work, that you may be perfect and complete, lacking nothing" (James 1:4). Lacking nothing! Wow--! After reflecting on that Scripture, I decided I want that type of completeness in my Christian life. What mountains could the Body of Christ remove if the church possessed that kind of godly perfection? Think about that! The church, once again, could turn the whole world upside down (cf. Acts 17:6).

When I speak of completeness throughout this book, I am speaking of the process of becoming spiritually mature. I believe spiritual maturity is the abundant life Christ spoke of in John 10:10 when he said this about his followers, "I have come that they may have life, and that they may have it more abundantly." John MacArthur in his commentary on John 10:10 wrote, "Only Jesus Christ is the one true source for the knowledge of God and the one basis for spiritual security." I believe that spiritual security is achieved in two ways: faith in Christ and spiritual growth. Without having the first part, it's impossible. Without the latter part, maintaining a vibrant Christian walk would be difficult--if not impossible.

When you examine the Apostle Paul's life, and consider the level of spiritual maturity he achieved and all he accomplished during his missionary journeys. The many epistles he wrote the churches he planted, and his willingness to die for Christ; you might think he had reached that perfect completeness. With all of those spiritual credentials, he still struggled. Paul may have been the most influential Christian leader, other than Christ, of the early church. Yet, he struggled, as we all do at times, with the question, why is it so hard to do the right thing when you know what the right thing to do is? Paul records his frustration in this area and comes to the conclusion that it is only through Christ's work on the cross we receive the stamp of perfection from God. Romans 7:18--25,

> For I know that in me (that is, in my flesh) nothing good dwells; for to will is present with me, but *how* to perform what is good I do not find. Now if I do what I will not *to do,* it is no longer I who do it, but sin that dwells in me. I find then a law, that evil is present with me, the one who wills to do good. For I delight in the law of God according to the inward man. But I see another law in my members, warring against the law of my mind, and bringing me into captivity to the law of sin which is in my members. O wretched man that I am! Who will deliver me from this body of death? I thank God—through Jesus Christ our Lord! So then, with the mind I myself serve the law of God, but with the flesh the law of sin. (Italics theirs)

Even after all Paul accomplished he describes himself as a wretched man: Definition: "someone to be pitied, existing in a state of hopelessness." I believe Paul understood how wretched a man he was without Christ's covering. He understood there was no way he could live a life without Jesus that would enable him to be in the presence of a perfect and holy God. Seeing ourselves as wretched is a good place to begin this journey to completeness: understanding that our invitation to stand before a holy God is possible only through a right relationship with Jesus Christ.

If you do not know Jesus Christ as your Lord and Savior remedy that right now. When Adam and Eve sinned, by disobeying God's commands, sin entered the world and infected every human being (cf. Romans 3:23). God's plan to rectify that situation was to send his son Jesus to die on the cross--shouldering all of humankind's sin upon his own shoulders. God is so holy he cannot look upon sin. That is why he looked away from Jesus as he hung dying on the cross (cf. Matthew 27:46, Mark 14:34). As the precious blood of Jesus Christ flowed from his body, it washed away our sins. As a result of that sacrifice, when God looks upon us he does not see our sin but he sees the righteousness of Christ.

The wonderful news is that this covering of Christ for our sins is free. God's grace cannot be earned, nor can you be good enough on your own merit to obtain it. All that is required of you to be righteous in the sight of God is to accept, by faith, the Lord Jesus for the forgiveness of you sins. It is as simple as ABC. In a simple prayer, confess to the Lord Jesus that you are sorry for the sins you have committed. Ask Jesus to forgive you of those sins, and give him permission to be the Lord of your life. Then begin to learn everything you can about this merciful, loving, kind, and forgiving God.

Chapter 1

My Youthful Encounter with Jesus

I cannot remember if it was late spring or early summer but I do recall it was a hot Sunday morning. I was squirming, while sitting on the hard wooden pews in the First Baptist Church in Greenfield, Indiana. I believe I was around ten or eleven years old. It was my normal practice to sit in the front pew while listening to the pastor. Why--I don't know. I was a fairly innocent boy at the time. I could only remember being beaten once by my dad, but I felt I deserved the beating for flunking the first grade. I now know that no one deserves to be beaten for any reason. If you are in a situation where that is happening, or experiencing any kind of abuse, speak to someone you trust right away who can help you.

My parents never took me or my sisters to church. But to their credit, they insisted on us going. I figured it was to get us out of their hair for a while. It is important for parents, especially in today's culture, not only to attend church themselves but to make sure their children go and experience the life-changing teachings available in the Scriptures. Everyone should have the knowledge of what is written in the Bible. How else can someone make an accurate assessment of its truth? Many people in today's culture shrug off the Bible because of what they perceive are in it or because of what someone has told them is contained in its pages. Too many hold onto the misguided belief that the Bible is not relevant in today's culture.

But the Bible is more relevant today than ever before, because the human race is more lost and confused today than at any time in history.

The stakes are too high not to find out the life-transforming message contained in the Bible. Most of America while I was growing up still embraced the teachings of the Bible, whether they went to church or not. Children were exposed to the teachings of the Scriptures in school, where they learned about prayer and were taught the existence of God and the significance of a relationship with him. That has changed considerably. In today's culture, according to the, *Christian Post*, 39 percent of adults from ages eighteen to twenty-nine have never read the Bible. I believe that today's lack of moral conduct, in America, is directly related to taking prayer and the teaching of the Word of God out of the school curriculum. And I am not alone. A Gallop poll found that 77 percent of Americans believe that the main cause of the decline in morals and values in the good old USA is a lack of reading the Bible.

Can this be a reflection on what is happening in our society today? Without the proper moral compass, as taught in the Scriptures, how can young minds discern what acceptable behavior is when it comes to moral issues? If America is ever going to stop the downward spiral of violence, addiction, and sexual immorality that quest must start with our children; we must educate them in the teachings of Christ and who they are in him. Young people need to understand there are consequences for disobeying the laws of the land and eternal consequences for disobeying God's law. If everyone around the world would follow the teachings of Jesus Christ, it would solve every problem the world faces today. Someday when Christ returns that will be the reality.

I believe too many Americans, especially the youth, are confused about who they are. It takes the understanding of the origins of human beings to comprehend who we are and why we exist on this earth. Children learn about the big bang theory and the theory of evolution in public schools but not the story of creation by an intelligent and loving God. Christians just want a level playing field in which to share their faith. My dad was an atheist and I was told over and over again that there was no God. I really tried to believe that but deep down in my gut I knew that was not the truth. In spite of my gut feeling, I tried to convince myself that it was true--failing to search out the truth for myself. I remember telling my cohorts that Budweiser beer and pot (cannabis) was my God. That is how deceived I had become. The more I slipped into darkness the more I tried to convince myself that there was no God. Living in darkness will do that to you. You become terrified of the light afraid someone might see the lost, scared person living inside you. But God knows that little child; and he loves you.

I am not an authority on the big bang theory or the theory of evolution and do not want to be; however, I have studied those theories--world views--while working on a college degree. After tossing those three creation choices around in my mind, the only one that made any sense was the story of creation; as told in Genesis. It is difficult for me to comprehend order coming out of a violent explosion. The earth was created in an orderly way with all the pieces fitting together in a system that meets all human need for survival. Contemplating the complexity of human life and human behavior, I found it simply did not make sense that human existence was started with an explosion or a single-celled creature crawling out of the ocean.

We must keep in mind that the big bang theory and the theory of evolution are just that—theories. They are not proven facts but postulations by human beings regarding how the world began. No one witnessed the big bang, nor was there one witness of the transformation of an ape into a human being. But there were over five-hundred eyewitnesses to the resurrection of the Lord Jesus Christ showing proof of his divinity. These were people who could have been put to death--and some were--for saying such things. But they came forward in spite of the danger and testified to this fact that they saw the risen Christ walking around after his death, "After that

He *"Jesus"* was seen by over five hundred brethren at once, of whom the greater part remain to the present, but some have fallen asleep" (1 Corinthians 15:6, italic emphasis mine).

Unlike the big bang theory and the theory of evolution the resurrection of Jesus Christ is well documented by eyewitnesses and recorded firsthand by the apostles. Who spent three years living with Jesus! There was no chance the apostles did not recognize Jesus after he revealed himself to them. The only logical assumption to explain the creation of the earth and its inhabitants was that it was done by an intelligent creator who put everything in its place for all of life to flourish.

How else can one explain the human heart: the complexity of the human heart and its ability to love and care for other human beings? And at the same time, how do you explain the depravity of the human heart; which embraces evil and has caused so much pain throughout the centuries? I have no way to explain the depravity of the human soul other than the fact that sin distorted God's intentions for humans to love as he loves--perfectly. I do know this. Love conquers all, and God's love will triumph over evil and restore humankind to fellowship with him.

Over the years, I have come to understand that there are only two things since the fall of humankind that have not changed. The Lord Jesus Christ and the extremes he went through to save humanity. And the depravity of the human heart and the extremes it will go to in order to get what it wants and achieve its evil desires, "Jesus Christ *is* the same yesterday, today, and forever" (Hebrews 13:8, italics theirs). "The heart *is* deceitful above all *things,* And desperately wicked; who can know it" (Jeremiah17:9, italics theirs). I believe those two truths are at the core of every human event and action in history. And will be the greatest factor in the future of human existence until the return of Christ.

How does the big bang theory or the theory of evolution explain the evil which exists in the world today? They don't! Nor do they profess there to be a remedy for that evil. Only the strong survive is not an acceptable solution to the evil that exists today and has existed throughout the centuries. That kind of thinking will only encourage more evil. A dog-eat-dog world philosophy will only create more mayhem and misery. I believe in spite of evidence to the contrary that humans *feel* an inward duty to take care of the weak in society--an inner knowing of what is right and wrong. And deep, deep down in their soul they desire to do what is right.

It has been evidenced over the centuries that humankind will never be able to resolve the evil that exists in the world without divine intervention. Look around. It is only getting worse. Without supernatural intervention the world will destroy itself, while evil will continue to proliferate with no end in sight. There must be an evil force causing such madness. The Bible teaches that you overcome evil with good, "Do not be overcome by evil, but overcome evil with good" (Romans 12:21). Jesus tells us that only God is good (cf. Matthew 19:17, Mark 10:17, Luke 18:19) and God is the only hope we have to defeat the evil forces dominating the world today. Only Jesus offers hope for tomorrow.

Within the confines of my pragmatic mind, divine creation and the fall of humankind is the only explanation for the emptiness of the human soul. Humans, continually, without success, I might add, try to fill their empty souls with every kind of polluted thing available on earth: alcohol, money, power, drugs, sex, food, and possessions. The complete list could fill volumes. None of those things satisfy the hungry soul. There is only one remedy for a starving soul and the human brokenness that seems to be even more prevalent in the world today. After years of struggling to find the answer, I now know the only answer to a soul's brokenness is the Lord Jesus Christ. Only Christ can create in a human a new heart, a new purpose, and a new hope, "I will give you a new heart and put a new spirit within you; I will take the heart of stone out of your flesh and give you a heart of flesh" (Ezekiel 36:26).

In order to change the depravity of the human heart, each individual, at some point in their life is in need of a heart transplant: a soft, loving heart that will replace a hardened heart full of selfishness, greed, anger, and hate. And transplant in its place a heart full of love, mercy, grace, and forgiveness. God has never lost one patient in all of his heart transplant procedures. And the operation is physically painless. However, the truth which the transplanted heart reveals can be painful when the Holy Spirit begins to reveal the hidden truths we try to hide about ourselves. When I finally surrendered my heart to Christ 100 percent, the cleansing tears of repentance flowed from my eyes for weeks. There is no shame in cleansing tears; they are the warm and comforting showers of the soul washing away all the shame and guilt that accumulates over the years.

Knowing God and serving him is not about a bunch of rules and liturgies. But about receiving the mercy, grace, love, and the joy of a changed life, which God wants to give to each human being. The *high* cost to accomplish that heart change was the death of God's only begotten son on the cross at Calvary. God wants your heart. A heart filled with love for Jesus and your fellow human beings is a heart God can shape and mold into his loving image: into the image of Jesus. A heart filled with hate, anger, and un-forgiveness is not a heart God can use. The human heart must be emptied of those evil attributes and filled with Christ-like attributes: love, joy, peace, kindness, mercy, and be a heart willing to forgive others.

If you look close enough, you will see the goodness of God all around you. In every breath you take, in every blade of grass and blooming flower you see. In every drop of rain that splashes on your face. With every twinkling star that shines so brightly in the evening sky, and every time a mother holds a new born baby to her chest. Such beauty could not have been painted by an explosion or a one-celled creature. It could only have been painted by a holy God with a heart and eye full of love and beauty.

America needs to return to its roots beginning with Genesis 1:1, "In the beginning God created the heavens and the earth." One of the most revealing and overlooked Scriptures in the Bible is Genesis 1:27, "So God created man in His *own* image; in the image of God He created him; male and female He created them" (italics theirs). Human beings were created in the image of God. They were created perfect and complete, but sinful rebellion (cf. Geneses 3) put an end to that completeness. After the fall, man put on an image of corruptible flesh. The great news is that God sent Jesus to make us perfect in His eyes once again. God created human's male and female each with their own role in propagating and preserving the human race. Common sense would dictate that the failure of male and female to carry out their God given blessing to go forth and multiply would cause all human and all animal life to cease--going the way of the dinosaur--becoming extinct, "You shall take with you seven each of every clean animal, *a male and his female*;" two each of animals that *are* unclean, *"a male and his female"* (Genesis 7:2, italics mine).

Even though my parents did not go to church, because they sent me I meet Jesus Christ there one sunny Sunday morning. While gazing up at the preacher, attired in black suit, white shirt, dark tie, and waving a King James Bible. The words he spoke that day penetrated my heart. The pastor began telling me about this man called Jesus, who lived hundreds of years ago. He spoke of Jesus' love for me and how Jesus sacrificed his life so I could be forgiven of my sins. Even at that early age, I had accumulated an impressive list of miscues. That morning I *felt* the Lord Jesus touch my heart. And without any reservations I gave my life to him. I did not completely understand the significance of what I had done, but I knew it was a good thing. After sharing this good news with family and friends, and receiving little encouragement to continue on in my new found faith. I deposited it in the back of my heart, where it stayed dormant for years.

Parents, if your child comes home and tells you that he or she has accepted Christ as Lord and savior--encourage them. Offer them your fullest support, regardless of your beliefs. Forcing your beliefs on your children will only confuse them. Allow their tender hearts to experience Jesus and his teachings, so they can make their own decision about its relevancy. Who knows, maybe, if you do not know the lord they will draw you to him. It happens all the time. "Out of the mouth of babes" (cf. Psalm 8:2, Matthew 21:16).

That Sunday morning was not the first time I had felt the Lord's presence. A few years earlier on Christmas Eve, while singing songs and celebrating Christmas with my sisters, I felt an overwhelming presence of God. I never told anyone about that experience, until now, but on that Christmas Eve I knew I had been touched by the Lord Jesus. I understood for the first time that there was a God in heaven and that he could be experienced on earth. I have never forgotten that night. I remember feeling such joy, peace, and love for others.

Coming from an abusive home, my life became chaotic and out of control. I searched and searched for the one thing that was going to fill the gigantic crater in my shattered heart. Deep down I knew alcohol was not an answer for filling the emptiness in a person's soul; but it numbed the pain for a short while. Alcohol, drugs, or any destructive habit is just a temporary escape or numbing of the pain. Eventually the pain returns and becomes unbearable and no amount of alcohol or drugs can make it go away. But the foolish heart keeps trying to drown out the horrible reality of its sorrow with the devils tools--without success. There have been times in my life, when I was so confused, I wished I would just die and get it over with. But God would have none of it, as I will share later in this book. I now know from my own personal experience that only Christ can fill the emptiness in the human soul and heal the pain of a broken life, "For He satisfies the longing soul, and fills the hungry soul with goodness" (Proverbs 107:9). The more I pursued the wrong things; the greater the black hole in my soul became. There was nothing perfect in my life except for how perfectly I messed it up. It is amazing how easily we can deceive ourselves into believing we have it all together.

Chapter 2

The Addiction to Alcohol and Drugs Begin

I began drinking when I was around ten or eleven years old. I remember sneaking over to a neighbor's house and stealing their home brew. I progressed from stealing home brew to having older folks purchase beer for me. I would take the illegally obtained beer down by the creek and proceed to drink the six pack of Pabst Blue Ribbon beer--one by one. In those early days, it did not take long for me to feel intoxicated and sick. I remember coming home sick as a dog and throwing up all over the window sill outside my bedroom. I still wonder how my parents never noticed the mess. Maybe they did.

Continuing into my teenage years, I began to hang around with some older guys who had cars. I remember riding around with them and getting wasted on orange vodka; talk about being sick. Soon I moved out of that small town never wanting to return. Today I live a few miles from the same small town--funny how that works. I was fifteen years old and working full time at a gas station on the west side of Indianapolis, Indiana with my dad. Since I made it extremely clear in the *Rising from Ashes* book how much I hated my dad. Maybe I should explain how I ended up working with him.

It was summertime time and my now brother-in-law, Larry, and I decided we wanted to go to Orlando, Florida for some fun in the sun and to check out the girls on the beach. We figured we could stay with my sister, Mary, who was living there at the time. We devised a plot to tell my sister, Nancy, who was dating Larry. After all, we did not want her tagging along, and we knew she would insist on coming. So we told her we were going to the laundry mat to get a coke and we would be right back. (Back then in a small town the laundry mat was about the only place open late at night with a coke machine.) After escaping, off we went to Florida in a 1953 Ford six-cylinder, 3 speeds on the column, with an overdrive.

After changing a flat tire and driving through the night, we found my sister's house in Orlando, Florida. After knocking on the door and discovering there was no one home; worn out from our tedious drive we returned to the car and fell fast asleep. Waking up the next morning, as we gazed outside, we noticed there was debris scattered everywhere. We later discovered we had slept through a hurricane (God was watching over us even then). After a couple of weeks in Florida we were broke, so dad sent money for all three of us to come home--with one condition. That I would go to work with him at a gas station in Indianapolis where he was working part-time.

I worked with dad for a couple of years and during that time I got to know him. I realized I loved my dad, and I was able to forgive him. I finally understood that he must have experienced a pretty tough childhood himself. Well, that is how I ended up working at a gas station, with my dad. Having my first full-time job was exciting. Best of all, it was right down the road from Speedway, Indiana famous for the Indianapolis 500 mile race. If things were happening in Indy, the west side was the place to be.

I worked in Indy for the next few years until I was drafted in 1970. Just my luck, in the selective service lottery my birthdate was drawn sixty-fifth. The question was not if I would get drafted, but when. The letter came, soon enough, and I prepared for the worse. The Vietnam War was blazing hot and protests against the war in America where heating up. My chances of going to Vietnam were pretty good. At the time I was drafted, I had a great job making good money as a route salesman. I really liked that job. I owned a nice car and had a new motorcycle. I was living a young man's dream. Living with my sister left me with few living expenses and responsibilities. I paid her twenty-five dollars a week for room and board and every Friday night she fixed me a steak dinner. For twenty-five dollars that was a bargain. I had it made. When the draft letter came, I had to sell the car, the motorcycle, and give up Friday night steak before leaving for basic training.

I did not want to be in the army. I was having too much fun as a civilian, but I felt it was my duty to serve my country. I loved my country very much then and I still do. Growing up I believed that America could do no wrong and that the leaders of this great nation were honest, hardworking, and had the best interest of the American people at heart. It broke my heart when I discovered how far that was from the truth. That discovery was a world-shattering experience for me. Sadly, it seems in today's society, it is accepted that corruption is part of the political system. When Watergate burst on the scene, I was shocked that criminal activity was instigated from the White House. For me that was the feather that broke the camel's back. (I am not going to take the time to explain Watergate, but if you want more information about it you can google it.)

The Watergate scandal added to my anger and distrust for the government and its leaders. I have since come to understand that people make mistakes, and the government is made-up of people. Many times well-meaning people believe they are doing what is right in their own eyes; when their true motive is fulfilling the desires of their own selfish heart. And we know how deceitful the human heart can be (cf. Jeremiah 17:9). Man's ways are not God's ways and even governments when they get away from the principles of life and government, as described in God's word; it swings open the door for corruption. And many race in not considering the consequences. But the Bible is clear, "You reap what you sow" (cf. Galatians 6:7).

After completing my training, I received my orders and they were for South Korea. Although the tensions were high in that country there was no actual combat going on. I found out, through the company clerk, that our original orders were for Vietnam, but had been changed at the last minute because our area of training was needed to replace a bunch of guys rotating out of South Korea. The war was supposed to be winding down and I was thankful for the change of orders. No one in my training company wanted to go to Vietnam in 1971. (I believe there were two guys in our company who volunteered for Vietnam.)

Over the years, I have often thought about how I was spared the horrors of Vietnam. I have never *felt* as if I was anyone special and I have often wondered why I was spared. Survivor's guilt plagued me as I read about the young men and women sacrificing their lives in the cities, rice patties, and jungles of South East Asia. But I never requested a transfer. I now find solace in the fact that I did honorably serve my country. I went where they ordered me to go and was willing to put my life in danger if that is what I was asked to do.

The guilt I *felt* for not dying in Vietnam only added fuel to the already fragile state of my mind. I like to think I was spared from going to war because someday I would have a story to tell about God's love, grace, faithfulness, and redemptive power that would help others who are struggling with addictions. My prayer is that this book is that story.

I was not physically strong and coming from an abusive back ground I had very little confidence in myself or my ability to survive such a terrible place. Did God spare my life? I believe he did. Over the years, there have been several times when God intervened rescuing me from a deadly situation. I am only going to mention a few of them for times sake. The first time I remember God rescuing me was at the Greenfield public swimming pool. I was just a young boy when I was playing in the shallow end of the water. Without realizing it, I drifted into the deep water. I began to go under once, twice, three times. I still remember the horror as I bobbed up and down as the water choked me and I struggled to breathe. Waving my arms and gasping for air was happening right under the life-guard's tower, but he never noticed I was drowning. I guess he had prettier things to look at than me. After going under several times, a woman grabbed me and guided me to the shallower end of the pool. She asked me if I was alright. I don't remember saying anything to her, but I know that woman saved my life. I have always felt God brought her to me. I told nobody about that scary experience, because I was afraid I would not be able to go to the swimming pool anymore. After that experience, I was careful to stay out of the deep end. And still today I am not a big fan of being in the water.

I can recall another time when God reached down from heaven and snatched me from death. I was twelve or thirteen years old and some of my friends and I decided to hitch-hike to Indy for the Indianapolis 500 mile race. The trek was about forty miles down highway 40 and to the north from where I lived in Greenfield, Indiana. That was a pretty long journey for a bunch of kids thumbing it. When we arrived at the White River, we approached a cement wall partly collapsed and partly standing. We began to cross on the collapsed concrete making our way to the standing wall. My friends were older than I was and physically stronger. They climbed to the top of the wall with little trouble. It was now my turn. As I began to climb, I felt my arms weakening and my grip slipping while trying to hang on. Panicking--I was losing my grip. Looking down I could see the water rushing below. (It was spring time in Indiana which brings a lot of rain and the banks of the White River were overflowing.) I knew if I fell into that powerful, fast moving water I would not survive. As we already know, I was not a good swimmer. One of my friends was stretching out to reach me from the top of the wall but was unable to grasp my hand. Then, suddenly, in a split second, I was standing on the top of the wall. Where this boost came from I did not know. All I know is that it was not because of my friend or myself; although, my friend was trying hard to reach me. Standing on the top of the wall we looked at each other, in disbelief, and shrugged our shoulders. After that the four of us headed to the track. I remember we had a good time, got sunburned, and later made it home safe. My friend and I never spoke of that event again. I know, without a doubt, it was the Lord or his angel that saved my life that day.

I believe in the existence of guardian angels. In the Scriptures angels are simply described as God's messengers. Angels are not meant to be worshiped. They are heavenly beings created by God just as we are earthly beings created by God. Not all angels are sent from God. Satan's henchmen (cf. 2 Peter 2:4) are fallen angels. The Bible teaches that humans were created just a little lower than the angels, "What is man that You are mindful of him, And the son of man that You visit him? For You have made him a little lower than the angels, And You have crowned him with glory and honor" (Psalm 8:4, 5). Just like angels, humans, in the right context are given glory and honor by God. Only God deserves to be worshiped (more on that in a later chapter).

There are numerous accounts of angels appearing to humans in the Scriptures (cf. Daniel 6:22, Matthew 28:2, Luke 1: 19, 28), just to name a few. The word angel in lower case appears 199 times in 190 verses in the NKJV version of the Bible (www.Blueletterbible.org). Angel when capitalized is referring to the King of Angels. Jesus. Jesus speaking to his disciples about the lost sheep of Israel emphasizes the importance of each of his little sheep. And warns those around him (and us) to watch what they do around these little ones because they have an angel to watch over them, "Take heed that you do not despise one of these little ones, for I say to you that in heaven their angels always see the face of My Father who is in heaven" (Matthew 18:10).

In the eyes of God, we are all lost sheep in need of a shepherd. In a human context, if you live to be ninety-nine years old and your child is seventy-nine years old. That child is still your baby. When Moses approached God at the burning bush--Moses was eighty-years old. Yet the conversation had the tone of a father talking to his scared and confused son (cf. Exodus 3, 4).

Through the many foolish and dangerous activities I did during my youth, and later while intoxicated; I felt someone was watching over me. I believed that someone was the only Christian man I knew growing up. That was my mom's dad. My grandfather spent hours praying for each one of his grandchildren. Grandpa was a kind and loving man dedicated to serving Jesus, the church, and his family. Grandpa went to be with the Lord in 1959. He was only 58 years old. After losing the only godly influence in my life, I now wonder how different my life might have been if grandpa had lived to help me become a man. A godly mentor in a young person's life is so important: a person who will model Jesus and explain the things of God as they are intended to be taught from the Bible. Without even seeking them out, there will be plenty of worldly mentors eager to plant their worldly philosophies in the mind and heart of a young person. If you are a truly godly person and feel the Lord calling you to mentor others, don't hesitate. The reward of watching God transform a young life into someone he can use to minister to others is worth its weight in gold.

Chapter 3

Striving for Completeness in Faith

Faith is the foundation of every Christian, and that foundation is built on Jesus Christ; the author and finisher of our faith (cf. Hebrews 12:2). The Bible teaches that without faith it is impossible to please God, "Without faith *it is* impossible to please *Him,* for he who comes to God must believe that He is, and *that* He is a rewarder of those who diligently seek Him" (Heb. 11:6, italics theirs).

In today's fast-paced society, where people expect instant everything, the definition of biblical faith as it pertains to the New Testament has lost its substance. The Holman Bible Dictionary says this about the watered down version of biblical faith in today's culture,

> The biblical concept of faith has been radically changed over the past century in theological and philosophical circles. These new definitions rarely address the complexities of the biblical concept, a concept in which the whole person, the physical world, God's word, and God Himself play crucial roles.

Biblical faith encompasses the whole person and is embedded deep in the heart and soul of each individual. Today there is a lot of talk about holistic healing. True biblical faith mixed with God's Word, a healthy life-style, and the power of the Holy Spirit can heal physically, emotionally, and spiritually.

Watered down faith quickly evaporates and leaves a person doubting the very existence of God, which is the same trick Satan used on Eve in Genesis chapter three. Before you cast God to the curb, and blame him for life's failures. Be sure your faith is a Christ-centered scriptural based faith. Anything else is a watered down version and will leave your soul thirsting for the true living water— Jesus Christ.

Through the years, people have put their faith in many things: people, a career, money, a 401 plan, a political party, and corporate America. But time after time all have proven to be at the whim of broken humanity and will eventually leave you wanting. True biblical faith is a hope of a better life to come, putting aside the flimsy hope offered by this world and placing your faith in the sure promises of an unchangeable God. Who loves you, will never leave you, or forsake you.

Jesus Christ never fails. If you have become disillusioned in your Christian walk it is not because Jesus has let you down it is your lack of commitment to him that has let you down. Americans love short cuts; but there is no short cut to a lively Christian life. Living a life that honors God takes hard work, wholehearted commitment, self-discipline, and becoming a student of the Bible. Jesus Christ never took a short cut to the cross to redeem us. He suffered every agonizing moment. Jesus felt each lash as it was tearing away at his flesh. He felt each blow of the hammer, driving the spikes deeper and deeper into his hands and feet. We owe Jesus our deepest commitment to live a life that witnesses to his love and commitment for us.

Christians are to live by faith, walk by faith, pray in faith, and overcome evil through faith. Faith is the very equilibrium of a Christian's life, "Now faith is the substance of things hoped for, the evidence of things not seen" (Heb. 11:1). God is intimately involved in the faith of each individual Believer through the physical world, through his word, and through the very presence of the Holy Spirit living in us. Faith is an interaction between us and God with Jesus being the go between. God actively cultivates and grows the faith he has given us. Brother Lawrence in his book, *The Practice of the Presence of God* said this about faith, "Instead of letting faith rule our lives; we are guided by our petty, every day, mechanical prayers, which are always changing. The churches only road to the perfection of Christ is faith."

Jesus describes faith as a tiny mustard seed in Matthew 17: 20 and Luke 17:6. A seed is something that is buried in the ground and through careful care grows to maturity and produces fruit. A seed needs good soil, water, and sunlight to grow. Faith in order to grow needs a commitment to Jesus, the Word of God, and the doing of good works. Good works is a sign of spiritual fruit as a Christian matures, "Faith by itself, if it does not have works, is dead. But someone will say, "You have faith, and I have works." Show me your faith without your works, and I will show you my faith by my works" (James 2:17, 18).

We are saved by grace. It is a free gift from God (cf. Ephesians 2:8). But good works is the process of actively living out our faith. Jesus showed the importance of doing good works while on earth. And we are to be Christ in the eyes of the world and without showing good works, in the name of Christ; the already blinded souls would become even more spiritually blind. Jesus cautioned his disciple that if the blind lead the blind both will fall into a ditch (cf. Matthew 15:14, Luke 6:39). As the church of Jesus Christ, we cannot crawl into our small social groups and ignore the needs of others. And the only way to help them with that need, whether physical or spiritual is to actively be seen as the Body of Christ doing good works in the name of Christ.

We need to be the optometrist for a world that seems to become more spiritually blind with every passing year. Let flickering eyes witnesses our faith in action so that our good works might open sightless eyes. Helping them avoid a tumble into a deep, dark ditch that few ever climb out of. I know that ditch exist, because I was stuck in it for so many wasted years. Yet, I know a wonderful savior is waiting to lower a ladder to the depths of despair so you can climb out of that ditch. Just raise your eyes toward heaven and cry out, "Help me Jesus!"

Jesus, not only by example, but by a calling, calls us to do good works, "For we are His workmanship, created in Christ Jesus for good works, which God prepared beforehand that we should walk in them" (Ephesians 2:10). Faith and good works woven together are needed--working hand-in-hand to reach the lost for Christ. A person's good works are a sign of spiritual maturity and demonstrates their willingness to give all they have for the furtherance of the kingdom of God on earth.

As in any spiritual discipline, you must do the necessary labor needed to grow your faith. We are to stand fast in our faith no matter what the circumstances; while waiting faithfully in anticipation of Christ's return. Do you see a hopeless situation surrounding you when you observe the madness spreading throughout the world--are you afraid? I think everyone is concerned. Paul's instruction to the church at Ephesus was to be brave and strong. He wrote in Ephesians 3:16, 17, "That we are to be strengthened with might through the Holy Spirit alive in the inner man that Christ may dwell in your hearts *through faith* that you be rooted and grounded in love" (italics mine). What does fear do to a Christian? Answer. It robs a Christian of their joy and causes them to worry and doubt the promises of God. It steals our faith! We stand steadfast in faith through the toughest times by the Spirit of God incarnate inside our hearts. Christian faith in its simplest form is trusting God to do what he has promised he will do, even though we don't see it at the time.

Do you fall apart when things get tough? Or do you strengthen yourself and others in the Lord? When a mature Christian's life gets hard, they stand firm abounding in faith. Persevering through the hard times is when our faith strengthens and grows. If our lives were without trials and tribulations why would we need faith? Will there be faith in heaven? Heaven will be the fulfillment of God's promise to his church—the perfect life. Looking into the eyes of Christ, there will be no need for faith. Because we would already have received the thing we now hope for--living in the presence of God forever. No more sorrow, no more pain, and no more tears. We confirm our faith in the eyes of others by showing love and grace in the worst of times. And we find joy in great trials of affliction furthering our witness of Christ's love for his church, "My brethren, count it all joy when you fall into various trials, knowing that the testing of your faith produces patience" (James 1:2, 3). And patience is a key element in the process of making us complete—spiritually mature.

Your faith will be tested and how you react to those tests reveals the strength of your faith. It is easy to have faith when times are easy. But tough to have faith when everything seems to be against you, but that is the time when our faith should be at its visual best for everyone we encounter to see, allowing them to recognize that it is our faith in Jesus Christ that gives us this amazing strength to persevere, arousing in their heart a desire to know such powerful faith, which only comes from a relationship with Jesus.

Saving Faith

What is saving faith? Answer. It is the planting of a small seed of faith, by God, in the heart of a man or a woman. And when nourished and watered by the Holy Spirit, and the Word of God—grows, and, grows, and grows. When such powerful faith is combined with sincere repentance it transforms into saving faith in Jesus Christ. This once tiny seed when given the right nourishment will develop into a mountain moving faith.

Christian faith grows through the understanding of the Scriptures. The better your knowledge and understanding of God's word the more your faith will blossom. It is within the pages of the Bible where we find answers to our questions about who we are, why we are here, who is Jesus Christ, and how do we relate to him? In the beginning, God put us on earth for his glory: creating us in his image, the beloved of all his creation. How terribly we let him down, "Everyone who is called by My name, Whom I have created for My glory; I have formed him, yes, I have made him" (Isaiah 43:7). Sin entered into the world destroying any glory found in mankind. But we are still God's beloved. So God sent Jesus to restore mankind's glory through faith in his son. Now our purpose is to share the good news of salvation through faith in Jesus to the entire world—the fulfillment of Jesus' command to evangelize the world brings glory to God.

Our Christian faith grows stronger through our prayer commitment. As we see God answer our prayers, our faith increases and enriches our relationship with Christ. Finally, we grow our faith through sharing Christ with others and observing the miraculous life-changes God cultivates in a born again person. The evidence of a changed life is quite a faith building experience; which I have personally witnessed while working in a biblical counseling and recovery ministry. I saw the miraculous changes God did in the life of others. And I experienced the astonishing changes God did in my own life. I cannot deny the miracle working power of Jesus Christ to change a person's life.

"Faith comes by hearing and hearing by the word of God" (Romans 10:17). One of modern time's great men of faith, Billy Graham, in his book, *Peace with God* wrote that according to the Scriptures faith will manifest itself in your life in three ways. In doctrine: in what you believe. In worship: your communion with God and in the fellowship of the church. And in morality: in the way you live your Christian life. I wholeheartedly agree with him, and would like to dig deeper into those areas as they pertain to faith in the life of a Christian.

Chapter 4

Striving for Completeness in Doctrine

Throughout this book when I speak of doctrine, I am speaking of the doctrine of God and Christ as taught from the Word of God. When it comes to sound doctrine, whom do you believe and what do you believe? Do you believe that the Scriptures are true and without error? Do you believe that Jesus died on the cross for the forgiveness of sins and rose from the grave three days later? Do you believe that Jesus Christ is the only way to heaven? Do you believe that you are saved by faith alone in Christ? For you to grow spiritually, it is crucial to understand the basic doctrines of the Bible. The more you read and understand the Scriptures the stronger your faith will become. I have heard it said that the Bible is God's love letter to his children, and everyone should know what is written in that love letter. For a Christian's faith to mature, they must have a sound knowledge and understanding of God's sacrificial love for them, the promises he has made, and the assurance of his return to earth to transport his people home.

The place to discover Christian truths are in the Bible: the doctrine of the origins of humankind, the fall of humankind, and the redemption of humankind. Paul warns his young pastor, Timothy, the time will come when people will no longer desire sound doctrine but will seek to fill their hearts with words that excuse their sinfulness, "For the time will come when they will not endure sound doctrine, but according to their own desires, *because* they have itching ears, they will heap up for themselves teachers; and they will turn their ears away from the truth, and be turned aside to fables" (2 Timothy 4:3, italics theirs).

Paul exhorts Titus to hold fast to the faithful Word of God as many scoffers will try to dispute what God has written distorting the Word of God for their own gain, "Holding fast the faithful word as he has been taught, that he may be able, by *sound doctrine*, both to exhort and convict those who contradict" (Titus 1:9, italics mine). In order to grow into spiritual maturity (completeness), you must be clear in your understanding of Christian doctrine, especially as the days grow shorter for Christ's return. Scoffers seem to be everywhere these days. Jesus, in revealing detail, warns us of the things to look for before his second coming in Matthew 24 and Mark 13. (If you have never read the Bible, or have read it sparingly, read those two chapters and decide for yourself if what Jesus describes in those passages sounds familiar when you consider the world we in live today.)

To live out our commitment to Christ we must experience Jesus for ourselves. That intimate relationship gives us the freedom and confidence to share Christ with others. How can you communicate to others about this life-saving savior if you do not know him intimately yourself? Where do we acquire this knowledge and understanding of God and his Christ? In the Scriptures, Psalms 119: 104 says, "Through your precepts I understand." Proverbs 2: 6 says, "For the Lord gives wisdom, and from His mouth come knowledge and understanding." The Scriptures are crystal clear. Knowledge and understanding come from knowing sound biblical doctrine. You can have knowledge without understanding; but you cannot have understanding without knowledge. You must seek out knowledge in order to gain understanding. The Bible, from Genesis 1:1 through Revelation 22:21 are all about the Lord Jesus Christ. Jesus said, "I am the beginning and the end the first and the last." The Scriptures teach us that all things exist through Jesus Christ and were created for him and by him (cf. Colossians 1:16).

God did not author the Bible so he could frighten you, control you, or prevent you from enjoying all life has to offer. The Bible was written to show you how much God loves you, how badly he wants to be part of your life, and how to make him the center of your life. God wrote his love letter to protect and save our lives--not destroy them.

Chapter 5

Striving for Completeness in Praise and Worship

Your faith will be evident in how important you make praise, worship, and communion with the Body of Christ. The Precious moments you spend in praising and worshiping Jesus is a sure indicator of how serious you are about developing your faith and demonstrates how serious you are about your relationship with him. Even though praise and worship energizes you and makes you feel good; its main purpose should be to bless God and demonstrate your love and awe of him.

When it comes to praise and worship, I have to admit that I have not completely understood their deepest meanings. But I am working on it. Are they different? If so, in what ways do they differ? Is praise and worship simply raising our hands and singing praise songs? Is it sitting in silence waiting for God to speak? Christians are often speaking of "praising God" and rightfully so. Not just humankind is commanded to praise God, but God's existence commands that all living creatures praise him, "Let everything that has breath praise the Lord" (Psalm 150:6).

There are three words for praise in the Old Testament Hebrew Scriptures: *yadah*, to give thanks, *zamar*, sing praise and *halal* (the root of *hallelujah*) which means to praise, honor, or commend - Got

Questions, https://www.gotquestions.org/praise-God.html. Those three translations contain the idea of giving thanks and honor to one who is worthy of praise. And the Lord Jesus Christ is certainly worthy of our praise.

The Book of Psalms is a collection of songs filled with praises focused towards God. Among that collection is Psalm 9, which says, "I will praise you, O Lord, with my whole heart; I will tell of all your marvelous works. I will be glad and rejoice in you; I will sing the praises of your name, O most high" (Psalm 9: 1. 2).

The world today is in desperate need for a positive change. If the church of Jesus Christ would rejoice in our savior like King David describes in that Psalm. Our lives and the world we live in would quickly change for the better. Amen? First, in this Psalm, David describes the intimacy by which we should render praise to God--with our whole heart. God does not want halfhearted praise from lukewarm Christians (cf. Revelation 3:16). I really have to question the sincerity of a part-time Christian regarding their faith and commitment to Christ. I am not judging anyone--I have struggled in my own Christian life. Only God can judge, because he truly knows a person's heart. But when you see someone attend church only when it is convenient for them: once a month or even less. Seldom do they talk about reading the Bible, praying, or what God is doing in their lives. Rarely do they serve at church, if ever. If you find yourself falling into that trap (Satan loves part-time Christians) reexamine your relationship with Christ and return to the Lord with your whole heart. When you stop doing the things necessary to grow spiritually, it does not take long to be pulled back into the sin filled life God rescued you from.

Jesus commanded us to love God with all of our heart, soul, mind, and strength. I believe we should be praising him with that same passion. Maybe the Body of Christ should let our hair down and shout out to God the praise that is due him. Fanatic people, at sporting events, will shout, jump up and down, and go crazy when their team scores. That is expected of them. But if that kind of passionate behavior is demonstrated within the confines of a church that congregation might be considered extremists, or part of a cult. Should we not be as excited about the salvation of a lost soul liberated from eternal death? As a football fan is about a touchdown; which has no real significance in the realm of the reality of the horrors that surround us?

Secondly, in this Psalm we are told to praise God for his wondrous works and for all he has done. Too often we lose focus on why God created all the beauty that surrounds us. He created the mighty oceans and mountains, the beautiful sunsets and sunrises, the glorious flowers of the field, the beauty of a soaring eagle, the beauty of smell, sight, touch, and the beauty of loving God and the beauty of the love of another human being. He created those things and more for us. And in the beginning he created a perfect world in which we could enjoy them. The saddest event in human history is when humankind said no to God and all that beauty, and chose his own way over God's way.

Thirdly, we are to praise God in the presence of others, "I will give You thanks in the great assembly" (Psalm 35:18, Hebrews 2:12). The Holman Bible dictionary said this about corporate and individual praise, "Corporate praise is to be carried out in an orderly manner. Praise is also firmly linked to an individual's everyday life." We are to gather together as the Body of Christ to praise God. As individuals we are to continue that praise in the way we live our daily lives. The sincerest and most influential form of Christian praise is living a life that honors God, "Therefore by Him let us offer the sacrifice of praise to God, that is, the fruit of our lips, giving thanks to His name" (Hebrews 13:15). Our individual and corporate lives should be a concert of praise to God. Sincere praise swings open the doors to heaven, allowing us to enter into the very presence of God. So we can experience his gentle, loving touch.

Finding Completeness In Worship

What about worship? Is it the same as praise? After all, they are spoken of in the same breath. The meaning of the New Testament Greek word for worship most often translates: "to fall down before or to bow down before." How does that differ from praise? Remember the three Hebrew translations for praise: to give thanks, to sing praise, and the word hallelujah (praise the Lord). Praise and worship are not the same. Praise does not include bowing before someone. However, there are similarities between the two: wholehearted worship, corporate worship and daily worship. Also apply to praise.

You can praise a person for their good works and their accomplishments. And Scripture backs that up, "Now I praise you, brethren, that you remember me in all things and keep the traditions just as I delivered *them* to you" (1 Corinthians 11:2, italics theirs). Paul praises the church in Corinth for actually maintaining sound doctrine. But you can only worship God! If you worship a human being or anything else on earth, in the sea, or in the heavens it is idolatry. Christian worship should only be directed towards God the all-knowing, all-powerful, omnipresent triune God. Worship is an interlocking mechanism connecting humanity to a divine deity where humans respond to that connection in a mutual loving way.

True worship stems from the very moment we first encounter the one true God. That is, at the very moment we collapse, falling on our faces before a holy God and cry out, "Forgive me Lord, I am a sinner." You must first experience a divine encounter with Jesus Christ before you can truly worship God with you whole heart. Jesus, speaking to the Lady at the Well tells her, "That God is a spirit and those who worship him must worship him in spirit and truth" (John 4: 24).

Worship directed towards God is done in unison with the Holy Spirt. Holy Spirit inspired worship separates itself from the things of this world. Wholehearted worship is projected from the inner most recesses of the human spirit--from deep down in the soul. Worship is internal, spiritual, an act of deepest love and respect for a God worthy of such worship. And should be done with every step we take; honoring God in everything we do.

Worshipping in the spirit has nothing to do with our physical posture: standing with hand's raised, knelling at the altar, lying prostrate on the ground, but all of those are acceptable if the heart is where the worship is radiating from. The Holy Spirit is the one who energizes worship. Because he is in essence glorifying himself, and he has a direct line to God the Father and the Lord Jesus Christ. All true worship glorifies the Father and the Son and radiates from the Spirit of God living in us. The nature of Christian worship is from the inside-out and has two equally important ingredients. We must worship wholeheartedly and allow the Holy Spirit to lead the worship.

To Sum up this chapter:

- We worship and praise God with our whole heart.
- We worship and praise God in the way we live our lives.
- We give God glory and praise for all he has done for us.
- We gather together to raise our voices in glorious praise and worship to God.
- We must worship God in spirit and in truth.

If you desire to go deeper read the story of the Lady at the Well in John 4:5--42. Imagine yourself as the person standing in the very presence of God and pay close attention to how the Lady at the Well reacted after this divine encounter. And visualize how you might have reacted while standing in the presence of Jesus. Write a letter to yourself explaining the significance of what Jesus taught this woman about the correct way to worship God.

Chapter 6

Striving for Completeness in Communion with God, the Church, and how we Live our Lives

Communion literally means to "share." The Latin word for communion is "com-mun-is" meaning: "participation by everyone." When I speak of communion, I am not referring to the breaking of bread and the drinking of wine as Jesus spoke of at the last supper, but I am speaking of the sharing of life with Christ and the church.

As we open ourselves up to the goodness and grace of God, we begin the process of communion with him through the indwelling of the Holy Spirit. God is no longer this unapproachable grandfather figure many pretend to believe he is. But he now radiates in our hearts as this glorious creator giving new life and spiritual gifts to his children. We begin to speak freely to him through our prayers and the Holy Spirit. Sharing (communion) with him our fears, our shortcomings, our hopes, and our newly acquired desire to live a life that pleases him, giving him permission to steer us in the right direction--towards Christ and his kingdom to come.

God already knows everything about us since he is omniscient: "all-knowing." It is not for God's benefit we confess these intricate feelings hiding deep within our soul, but for our help. Empowering us to see how hopeless our lives are apart from fellowship with God. When we commune with God, we feel his presence, which arouses deep feelings of trust and love for him. Craving God's love keeps us on the right path, steering us toward communion with him forever, and awakens us to hear God's still small voice as he speaks words of love and encouragement in our ears. While communing with God, we feel the warmth of his love, which warms and embraces us through the coldest nights and hardest struggles.

Our Christian faith provides a better understanding of who God is and how we fit into his plans, and how we can assist him in bringing the kingdom of heaven to earth. It beckons us to share the message of redemption, through Christ, to anyone who will listen. The story of God does not end when our lives on this earth are over. It just begins. And it will be a much easier transition the better we know God. We will be at peace when the time comes to say good-bye to this world. That kind of peace can only emanate from an intimate relationship with Christ. If I must die, let me die in the grace and love of Christ, not consumed by the sins of the world.

Striving for Completeness In Your Daily Christian Life

The sincerity of someone's faith will be demonstrated in how they live their lives. Do they have a strong moral code; are they living a life that is pleasing to the Lord? Always remember that the first goal in a Christian's life is to please God (cf. Matthew 3:17, 2 Corinthians 5:9).

The devil is also involved in our daily lives and will go to any extreme to derail you from the path God has set you on. He wants to see you crash and burn with him and his henchmen. In the process of your daily walk, your enemy will try his best to damage your witness for Christ. Daily living for Jesus is the best witness a Christian can use to reach the lost. Be on guard for the devils tricks. Jesus cautioned us to be on the lookout for wolves in sheep's clothing. He also told us how to recognize them. By their fruits: how are they living their lives, "Therefore by their fruits you will know them" (Matthew 7:20). Do not fall prey to a wolf in sheep's clothing. There are more of them out there than you realize, and they are well disguised.

Living out your faith in a way that honors Christ is so important for spiritual growth, creating a snowball effect: your faith grows bigger and stronger each day. Esteeming Jesus in every detail of your life reveals Christ to others. Jesus must be the focus for every decision you make and in everything you say and do. Ask yourself this all-important question before you make any decision. Is what I am thinking, about to say, or about to do, pleasing to God? If the answer is no, don't do it, don't say it! Your actions define the person you are and the person you are going to be. Do everything as if Jesus is watching--because he is.

Someone once told me, "You may be the only Jesus someone sees." When you are at work, driving in your car, or standing in line at the grocery store are you modeling Christ to others, or are you hiding a sheep in wolves clothing? The greatest witness to those who do not know Christ is how well you reveal him to them in your everyday actions. Do others see Christ when they look at you? Sadly to say, fallen folks like you and me, until Christ returns, are the only Jesus the lost people on earth will see. No matter what the world throws at us. No matter how gloomy things might appear. Hold on to your faith by holding on to the love that Christ has for you,

> That Christ may dwell in your hearts through faith; that you, being rooted and grounded in love, may be able to comprehend with all the saints what *is* the width and length and depth and height— to know the love of Christ which passes knowledge; that you may be filled with all the fullness of God. Now to Him who is able to do exceedingly abundantly

above all that we ask or think, according to the power that works in us, to Him *be* glory in the church by Christ Jesus to all generations, forever and ever, Amen (Ephesians. 3:17--21, italics theirs).

If you wish to go deeper, read Hebrews chapter eleven and answer these questions:

1. Who or what are you putting your faith in?

2. While striving for completeness in faith, what have you learned from this chapter that can help you strengthen your faith?

3. Write down what your faith means to you, and how you have seen faith work in your life and in the lives of others. Put together a plan on how to grow in your faith.

Chapter 7

Born Again: A Life Transformed

Through the years, there were times when I tried to get right with God, but after a short while I ended up diving right back into the same murky river of sudsy foam I escaped from so many times before--repeating the cycle of addiction. In this chapter, I will share with you the life-changing moment when I cried out to Jesus for help. When you are stuck in the bottom of life's muddy quarry, there is no way out except to look up. I was at that point in my life. God does not desire to, but in order to save our souls he will allow us to experience the consequences of sin. Sin always results in poor decisions and fuels a life of hopeless futility. It is painful but God will allow hurtful circumstances if that is what it takes to rescue us from ourselves--saving us from eternal destruction (cf. Luke 15: 11-30, The Prodigal son).

After coming to the agonizing realization my life and family were dissolving before my eyes, while in a drunken stupor, I cried out to the Lord to rescue me. I was on my third marriage. (In this account of my life, and out of respect for my x-wives and their privacy I will not use their names, but will refer to them as broken relationship #1, #2, and #3.) One day when broken relationship #3 came home and said she was going to move in with her parents, I was dumbfounded. I thought things were going pretty well. A year and a half before that I had stopped drinking. It takes a powerful event to motivate a chemically addicted person to stop such a strong addiction on their own.

On my day off, I would spend the day down at the lean-too drinking. One particular day I was there drinking long into the night. When I decided to stager to the house, I found the front door locked. I was so intoxicated, even with a key, I could not figure out how to get the door unlocked. So I started pounding on the door and screaming until broken relationship #3 finally let me in. In my drunken rage, I told her and the kids to get out of my house. Unless you have seen a furious drunk in action it is hard to visualize the evilness that pours out of that person. As I was raging at the family, I looked at my young son, who was only three years old, and I saw a look of terror and disbelief in his eyes that shook me to the very core of my soul. I could not get his sweet little face out of my mind. It haunted me. That episode made me realize the damage I was doing to him and to the entire family because of alcohol.

My family returned home shortly after that horrible night. But a short time later broken relationship #3 moved out again--taking my young son with her. I was broken hearted. Her exodus sent me reeling; and I went on a nine month drunk which broke all previous records. (I remained sober every other weekend when I had my son.)

I love my children. But my youngest son was special because it gave me a second chance to be a good dad. I love my first son with all my heart; but I was a terrible dad to him. I never abused him physically. I only spanked him once that I can recall, but I abandoned him which is just as painful for a child. I prayed to God for another chance at being a dad. I believed my youngest son was the second chance I prayed for. I could not figure out why God was allowing this breakup to happen.

Towards the end of my nine month drunk I realized that if my life did not change soon I was going to perish. My normal routine was to get plastered on the weekend when I did not have my son; and listen to rock and roll music as loud as it would go. On this particular night, I was outdoing myself in the art of intoxication while listening to the Rolling Stones album Sticky Fingers. Even in the grip of a drunken stupor, I saw clearly, for just a moment, and realized that everything in my life which I loved was slipping away from me. My eyes filled with tears, I cried out, "Jesus, I need you," and again "Jesus, I need you." Those words echoed through the house over the screaming guitars and the pounding of the drums shrieking from the stereo in demonic rhythms. Was that my voice--"I asked?" Surely it was mine. I was the only one here. Finally, and mercifully, I passed out, waking up in the recliner the next day. I tried to remember what happened the previous night. Did I cry out to Jesus for help, or was it just a dream? Only time would tell if Jesus heard me and how sincere I was in my plea for help.

I welcomed the next morning hungover; complete with a throbbing headache and a horrible upset stomach. Even so, I knew there was something different about me. I could not put my finger on what it was, but I was different. My life-situation had not changed, but I had. After beginning my renewed life in Christ, I came across this quote from A.W. Tozer, "It is doubtful whether God can bless a man greatly until he has hurt him deeply." I felt the sting of that kind of pain many times in my life and I believed that someday God was going to use me to help minister to broken people.

Shortly after my conversion, broken relationship #3 and the kids came home and things seemed to go well for a while. We started attending church as a family and got involved in Christian ministry. But a short six years later I got the greatest challenge to my faith and sobriety. Broken relationship #3 came home and told me she did not want to be married to me anymore and left again--taking my young son with her. I was so angry. Sitting on the couch, disgusted, my thoughts ran wild. "God, why are you allowing this to happen?" "After all, I have been doing my best to serve you;" "I am no longer living a life of rebellion and drunkenness." While sitting there, my thoughts went to drinking again. It was the middle of the week; so I made up my mind that this coming weekend I was going to get a 12-pack of beer and get wasted.

The devil is extremely evil. He will do anything and everything to destroy your faith in Jesus. And that includes using people to accomplish his goals. Everything is not always going to go your way. It is critical to hold on to your faith during times of trials and tribulations. I assure you they are going to come. It is at these crossroads that a powerful faith will make the difference between giving in to temptation and being victorious over it. The devil loves to kick Christian's when their down and I felt him stomping on me unmercifully. I could visualize, at times, the devil walking away with a cynical grin on his face, laughing, thinking he has gotten the best of me. I hate him.

Going to work was difficult. Trying to conceal the hurt I felt from co-workers was hard. We were pretty close. The mind, the mind, the mind, what evil tricks it plays on you--if you let it. When the devil attacks in a hurtful situation, the battle for your soul is raging. That is when faith in Christ, prayer and Bible knowledge will carry you through. Put on the whole "Armor of God," "Above all, taking the shield of faith with which you will be able to quench all the fiery darts of the wicked one" (Ephesians 6:16).

The mind controls the heart and the heart controls our actions. The heart and mind are inseparable when it comes to controlling your actions and defining the type of person you are going to be. King David, said it well, "Examine me, O Lord, and prove me; try my mind and heart" (Psalm 26:2). Jeremiah said this of the Lord, "I, the Lord, search the heart, I test the mind, even to give every man according to his ways, according to the fruit of his doings" (Jeremiah 17:10). The mind, the heart, and the doing are actually one. When we become one with Christ, he becomes the rightful owner of both the heart and mind. Attacks from the enemy are going to come, especially when you are dealing with life's problems. But remember the victory is yours; Jesus won the victory for you on the cross when he defeated Satan. Continue to resist the devil and he will flee from you, James wrote, "Therefore submit to God. Resist the devil and he will flee from you" (James 4:7). Submit your heart, mind, and actions to God and trust him to protect and guide you.

As the weekend approached, I began to think about all Jesus had done for me. How much I loved him and how much he loved me. I thought about the prospect of crawling on my belly, once again, in the mud where Jesus found me a few years earlier. I realized I had to cling to Jesus no matter how difficult life's struggles became. There were times when I felt I was grasping him around his ankles and toes holding on for dear life. Well, it was a struggle, but I made it through that first weekend sober, and the next, and the next, and the next. One of the thoughts I could not shake during that time was that I would break Jesus' heart if I started drinking again. I could not bear the thought of hurting him; after all he had done for me.

Jesus was asked what the greatest commandment of all was. His answer, "To Love the Lord your God with all your heart and with all your soul and with all your mind and with all your strength" (Mark 12:30). Love is the strongest of emotions, "For love is as strong as death" (Song of Solomon 7:6). God created the world in love and sent his only son to die for our sins because he loved us. Our love for Christ is the strongest umbilical cord we have to attach us to him. Nothing will help you persevere through trials, tribulations, and temptations more than your love for Jesus. Tell him often how much you love and need him, but most importantly, show him how much you love him by successfully living out your faith through your obedience to him.

Chapter 8

The Ugliest Years

Before I share with you the wonderful things Jesus has allowed me to experience, since surrendering my life to him. I want to share with you the worst years of my life. Even as a youth I had a tendency to drink. Being alone in a foreign country energized that desire to get intoxicated and escape. And it soon took control of my life. In a non-combat zone, being in the army after completing training was like having a 9--5 job. You would execute your duties during the day time. And on occasion you would have weekend duty or be out in the field. But your evenings and most of your weekends were free to do what you wanted. Honestly, one of the major struggles I had with military life was boredom. I began to drink more and more--my excuse--what else is there to do. In reality the army offered a lot of activities you could do instead of drink, and many soldiers took advantage of those opportunities. I wish I had. But drinking alcohol and smoking pot was how I chose to spend my time.

I was introduced to pot the first night in Korea. I did not see what the attraction was at first. The first time I smoked pot I did not feel any different. There were three groups of people in our barracks: the drinkers, the stoners, and the neither's. When I first got to Korea, I could not understand the stoners. All they wanted to do was get high. I thought what a waste. Early on I kept my drinking restricted to the evening hours and weekends and I smoked pot on occasion.

But it did not take long before I was smoking pot all the time, even during the day. I soon became like peas in a pot with the stoners; I wanted to get high all the time. There has to be a lesson in there somewhere about judging others.

After combining alcohol and pot and becoming disillusioned with the high, in order to get a more powerful high I began to experiment with harder drugs, such as LSD and other hallucinogen's. Cocaine, speed, downers, and prescription drugs were all part of my quest for that perfect high. The artificially induced ultimate high never comes. Chemically produced feelings of peace and joy, brought on by alcohol, drugs or any destructive habit will be short lived. Such false god's quickly dissolve away leaving only emptiness, sorrow, devastation, and a frantic desire to begin the search all over again; in a futile attempt to relieve the constant pain that grows stronger and stronger each day--yanking you further and further away from reality. Trying to find what only Jesus can offer drives the hurting soul to continue its pointless search to no avail--drowning you in loneliness and despair. As we learned earlier, only Jesus can restore peace and joy to a broken spirit. Drugs were a large part of my addictive behavior, but as I got older and more paranoid I stop using illegal drugs. Alcohol remained my drug of choice and continued to wreak havoc in my life.

I survived the army with an honorable discharge and after returning home I sought out fellow stone-heads so I could have some companions and a source for my addiction. It was not long before alcohol and drug addiction took complete control of my life. During that time I was a horrible person. Although, I did not see myself that way, but that description fit me perfectly: I was selfish, self-serving, and self-absorbed. I perfected the art of taking advantage of anyone and everyone to get what I wanted. At every family get-together I would get as drunk as I could and make a complete fool out of myself (described today as acting out). And in the process hurting one of the kindest people I knew and truly loved, my mom. My precious mom went to be with the Lord in December, 1987. My dad also died that month and year. What a heartbreaking time that was for my family--burying mom and dad just a few days apart. And it was Christmas. My parents had been divorced for several years when they died so close together. It makes you wonder, doesn't it?

My destructive life continued destroying everything in its wake. Bars became a regular thing for me. Getting drunk and seeking out drugs was all I cared about. I am amazed that I survived those years. There were several times in bars when I was totally out of control and could have been shot or stabbed, which happened in those places on occasion. And the times I met with strangers, in a secluded place, to buy drugs. But I survived and I believe that the Lord had a hand in protecting me.

One incident sticks out in my mind. I wrote in an earlier chapter when the Lord protected me from death or injury. On another occasion, I was drinking at a bar where I got totally out of control. I was bothering this young woman in the bar when some guys came to her rescue and made me leave. I staggered to my car and fell asleep, or more accurately; I passed out. Low and behold, I woke up the next day looking out my apartment window. Broad Ripple was some forty miles from my apartment in Greenfield. Staring out the window, I could not recall how I got home. I did not know anyone at that bar who could have or would have driven me home. And where were they, if they had? I could not remember driving or what route I took. I totally blacked out after leaving the bar and passing out in the car. An alcoholic blackout is defined as, "A form of amnesia in which a person has no memory of what occurred during a period of alcohol abuse and intoxication." - Mosby's Medical Dictionary 9th edition. If you have experienced an alcoholic blackout, or you drink until you are totally out of control there is help available to you. Seek God's help, start attending church and seek out a recovery ministry in your community. Celebrate Recovery and AA is two viable places to go for help and support in your desire to live a life of sobriety.

The sight of seeing my car out front and not knowing how it got there was a scary moment. For the first time, I realized how far from sanity I had withdrawn. I have wondered over the years who or what drove that car home. I am sure of one thing; I did not remember doing it. I believe the Lord intervened on my behalf and got me home without killing myself or someone else. That episode defined my life for so many years. So many of those years are a blur to me; maybe that is a blessing in disguise. My sister, Nancy, tells me things I did that I do not remember doing. It is like she's lying to me, but I know she's not.

During those ugly years I had a complete moral breakdown. I stole, I lied, and I used people for my own gain. Whatever deceitful activity it took to feed my addiction I was willing to do. I think about those years and feel ashamed. As I look back, I want to believe it was someone else performing such awful deeds--but it was me. I feel I came close to the point of no return during those years. So close to complete insanity, hopelessly lost, never being able to find my way back to reality. I know God has forgiven me, but I still scratch my head sometimes and wonder what in the world happened to me. How could a young boy from a small Indiana town end up so depraved? Humans have the uncanny ability to deceive themselves into believing that their sinful actions are justified. Have mercy on us all--Lord Jesus.

Oh despicable me. What a heartbreaking moment it was when I realized how depraved I had become. A shattered, untamed heart is a dangerous weapon. It can wreak havoc on an unsuspecting world destroying everything and everyone in its path. I have come to understand that the moment one comprehends how depraved the human heart really is. Is the moment they have that eye opening insight on how much they need a savior. And God willing they realize that savior is the Lord Jesus Christ. No other name can do what Jesus can do: to create in you a new heart and give you a new purpose. In my own eyes, surviving those years was truly a miracle from God. There is no other way to explain it. I wrote a poem explaining how I felt during that time.

The Stranger in the Mirror

The pain of my past I can't seem to shake;
Sometimes my life seems so fake.
Drawn to the things I shouldn't do, I run to my addiction;
I'm destroying my family with all this friction.
Family and friends, who are they to say;
I just want my drink; I hope they go away.
I'm not hooked, I can quit anytime,
I'm not a drunk, I'm in my prime.
I don't care what people say, this isn't denial;
it's just my articulate style.
The pain of my youth I've tried to drown,
But drink after drink it's still around.
One too many, is just a cliché!
I'm drunk again; last night, what did I say.
The morning sun shines in my room so bright,
can't open my eyes that face in the mirror it looks a fright,
Someone I don't know stares back at me.
Through the door, I hear my son say, "are you ok daddy?"
What did I say and what did I do.
Where is my family, now they're gone too?
Someone please help me my life is out of control,
I've been told the cross of Christ is where I should go.
One step, one day at a time.
One giant leap towards Jesus, now that doesn't rhyme;
They tell me that Christ died to set me free,
Thank you, Lord Jesus for saving me.

Chapter 9

Broken Relationships: Lives Shattered

Human relationships are one area, and maybe the most difficult, where we need to strive for completeness in our Christian walk. I cannot blame anyone except, me, myself, and I for the broken relationships I have destroyed. Three failed marriages and one relationship where I had a child out of wed-lock clearly shows how inept I was at relationships. One of the most painful experiences I have had was when that child died of pneumonia six months after he was born--brought on by "osteogenesis imperfecta," or "brittle bone disease." Ronald Wayne was born with two broken legs and two broken arms. I only saw him once when I went to a children's ward at Wishard Memorial Hospital in Indianapolis, Indiana, a state run facility. I was not able to hold him because of the possibility of breaking one of his bones. My mother was the only other person in my family to see him. Hospitals were quite different in those days. I can remember walking around that place observing the children in that ward. That was the saddest place I have ever experienced. There was a young boy with an enlarged head that still sticks in my mind to this day. I will never forget the look in his eyes as our eyes met. It seemed as if he was pleading to me for help. I had to turn away. I could offer him no hope, what an empty feeling that was. But that empty feeling never woke me up to the realities of life and what are really important—people (relationships). It took Christ and years and years before that wakeup call penetrated my hardened heart.

As usual, my cowardly reaction to the birth of my young son was to run as far and as fast as I could to avoid taking any responsibility for him or his mother. Shortly after he was born I was drafted, which allowed me to rationalize in my mind that abandoning them was not my fault.

Every relationship I entered into, no matter how short, was to get out of it something for myself. After the Lord delivered me from alcohol, I had so many relational issues to deal with; although, I would not admit that at the time (denial). While drowning in denial, I refused to believe I needed recovery in the area of relationship. I carried a lot of baggage around besides chemical addiction. A short list: selfishness, pride, anger, greed, isolation, and the belief that I came first and everyone else could fall in line behind my wants. Now maybe you can begin to perceive why I have been divorced three times.

Broken relationship # 1 is one of the sweetest, kindest people I have ever known. So, naturally, I took complete advantage of the relationship. Needless to say, my first marriage ended quickly. A few years back, I was able to ask her to forgive me. Her answer, "Jim, I forgave you years ago." So good to hear those three little words--I forgive you. Forgiving and receiving forgiveness will go a long way in the process of spiritual and emotional healing. Those three little words, when spoken sincerely, open the door for brokenness to begin to heal and allow someone to move forward in their recovery (More on forgiveness in a future chapter).

I ran like a gazelle from every commitment; scared to death I might have to give something of myself to someone else. I was not willing to give up what I believed was freedom, but the freedom I thought I had was really a self-made prison complete with invisible bars and locked doors, which was, actually, harder to break out of then Alcatraz. Do not accept a life-long sentence of addiction; seek the chain breaker Jesus Christ for a pardon.

During the ugliest years of my life I met broken relationship # 2. I am a pretty stubborn person and when I was told not to see her again; I could not help but see her. The two of us ran off to Las Vegas and got married. After returning to Indiana, we soon realized what a terrible mistake we had made. So much of those years are a blur to me because of alcohol and drug use. I do not remember much about our marriage, except how mean and hateful I was to her.

We are down to broken relationship # 3. Except for family members this was the longest sustained relationship of my life. I was shocked when things did not work out in my third marriage. But I must take full responsibility for all three of those failures. According to the teachings of the Bible, it is the responsibility of the husband to keep love flowing in the home and in the marriage. I did not do that. Emotionally and physically I separated myself from broken relationship # 3 and the kids. Early in the marriage, I participated sparingly in family activities because I wanted to be alone so I could get drunk. After coming to Christ, the reason I did not spend time doing things as a family was because I was a selfish, self-centered person, and I wanted to do what I wanted to do. The apostle Paul wrote in Ephesians 5, "Husbands, love your wives, just as Christ also loved the church and gave Himself for her, that He might sanctify and cleanse her with the washing of water by the word" (Ephesians 5: 25, 26). In this Scripture, The Lord clearly commands the husbands to love their wives: to put the wife's needs before their own.

Truthfully I never knew what the spiritual and emotional needs of the other family members were, because I was only concerned about them meeting my needs. In order to keep harmony in the family, it is crucial for you to find out the needs of your spouse and children and then do your best to meet those needs. Earning a living and meeting the physical needs of the family is important. But the other needs are just as important. Something that seems trivial to you might be of utmost importance to your wife and children. Do not be afraid to ask them about their spiritual and emotional needs and what you can do to help them satisfy those needs. You will not be able to meet ever need, but when family members know that you did all you could to meet their needs. They will feel safe to share their needs, wants, and dreams with you in the future.

Keeping Love Alive In the Marriage

I want to remind husbands that on the Day of Judgment you will be judged by a higher standard as head of the household, because you have been commanded by God to sacrifice for your wife and family. Even to the point of giving your physical life for them if necessary. Husbands it is important to understand that there is more to giving your life for someone then physically dying for them. The most essential sacrificing for your family comes from how you treat your wife and family on a daily basis. This requires that you give them your sacrificial love, you give them your time, you show them kindness and understanding, and you provide for their physical needs. Just offering your wife a shoulder to cry on and helping out with the kids and the housework will go a long way in keeping love alive in the home. When you help out around the house, this allows your wife some well-deserved alone time. And relieves some of the stress that comes when the woman of the house feels she has to do it all.

Scripture teaches that it is the responsibility of the husband to present his wife and family to the Lord holy and without blemish (cf. Ephesians 5:26, 27). Is that a monumental task? It is. And to accomplish that command takes complete commitment to God's word and relying on the power of the Holy Spirit. Husbands, embrace the command to be the spiritual leader of the home. It is God's design for the family. You will make mistakes, as we all do, but learn from those mistakes and press on. Do not let doubt creep in. Or allow the devil to convince you that you are not equipped to be the spiritual leader of your home--you are. God will give you everything you need to fulfil that role if you allow him to do so.

Dad's set the example: be the first one up and ready for church on Sunday morning, pray with your family often, take time to read and discuss the Bible with them, host small groups and Bible studies making sure the family gets involved. And always be available to answer any questions they might have.

Not only is it your responsibility to keep love blooming in your marriage. But in order to do that you must work diligently at keeping romance alive in your marriage. Bring your wife flowers and candy for no reason. Drop the kids off at moms and fix your wife a romantic candle light dinner, or take her on a date night. Never stop telling your wife how much you love and need her. Tell her repeatedly how valuable she is to the family and what a great wife and mother she is.

God loves romance and encourages it between a husband and a wife. I recently reread Song of Solomon from the Old Testament and for the first time I saw the beauty of it. How deeply the two loved and longed for the presence of each other. How unashamedly they shared their passionate love for one another; how they poured compliments on each other, and how they could not wait to be together again. Guys remember when you first fell in love with your wife and how you thought about her all day long and could not wait to see again; keep those feelings alive.

I do not believe that Solomon is writing about a sexual encounter type of love, which in the confines of marriage God blesses. But I believe he is writing about a deep, deep love that can only happen within the very depth of the hearts of two people. Fulfilling God's plan for marriage: the two becoming one flesh and sharing the innermost thoughts and feelings that two people can have for each other (cf. Genesis 2:24).

A Word To the Wives

Wives help your husband keep love and romance alive in your marriage. Paul ends Ephesians chapter five with, "Wives respect your husbands." While doing marriage counseling, I found a reoccurring problem in struggling marriages which was two-fold. The wife did not *feel* loved and the husband did not *feel* respected. I think we can sum this chapter up by saying; wives love and respect your husbands and husbands love your wives with a sacrificial love. Men make sure love is flourishing in the home. Ladies respect your husband and give him the freedom and confidence to be the spiritual leader of the home.

There is no pecking order between husband and wife. God created both male and female equally; although, their responsibilities to God and each other are different, "He created them male and female, and blessed them and called them *"Mankind"* in the day they were created" (Genesis 5:2, italics mine). God created both male and female and defined them as one: "Mankind" erasing any assumed differences between them.

The inequality began at the time of the separation between God and mankind--at the fall. It was sin that broke the fidelity of the male and female relationship (cf. Genesis 3:16, 17). It is Christ who restores unity to the male and female relationship. In Christ's church, there should be no feeling of superiority by male or female; both are equal in the sight of God. God will use either male or female in a powerful, powerful way, not because of gender, but because of their love and commitment to him.

A marriage between a husband and wife modeled after God's design for marriage and covered in Christ-like love will produce children with godly character. Godly parents produce godly homes which will increase greatly the percentage of children saying no to the destruction that awaits them in the fast-paced society we live in. Train up a child in the way *he/she* should go, and when *he/she* is old *he/she* will not depart from it" (Proverbs 22:6, italics mine). Giving children a chance to grow and have a good life begins with the atmosphere you create in the home: husbands love your wives, wives respect your husbands.

I understand that parents can do everything right and still have a child that goes astray. If that happens, know in your heart that you did everything in your power to bring them up in the knowledge of Christ. While they are out trying to figure out life on their own, take comfort knowing that you have planted a strong foundation of faith in their heart and someday when they come to their senses, like the Prodigal Son, they will return to the Lord and to you. Amen! While they have gone astray, guard against feelings of false guilt that can creep in. Once a child reaches a certain age they make their own decisions and are accountable to God for those decisions--not you.

If you desire to go deeper: read the book of Ephesians paying close attention to the verses on marriage and family relationships. Then inscribe a letter to yourself, or make a list, emphasizing the areas in which you need to improve in order to be a better husband, wife, and parent. Write a letter to yourself on how you can use this biblical instruction to enrich the relationships you have and set guide-lines on how to maintain those relationships in a way that honors God.

Chapter 10

Striving for Completeness in Relationship

Maintaining positive relationships may be the hardest of the biblical disciplines we face. Having to deal with others in a fallen world brings some real challenges, especially if the other person does not have a relationship with Christ. With that being said, the first relationship that is vital to get right is our relationship with Jesus Christ. If that relationship is not right all other relationships will be a struggle. It is upon the strong foundation of a relationship with Christ that gives us the platform in which we can build on all other relationships. The good news is that getting right with Jesus is the easiest relational step there is. The gospel, even as complicated as some try to make it, is very simple and easy to understand, "For whoever calls on the name of the *LORD* shall be saved" (Romans 10:13). It is that simple. Simply acknowledge you sins, request that Jesus forgive you of those sins and give him permission to take charge of your life. Once you have accepted Jesus Christ he sends the Holy Spirit to teach you, to guide you, to comfort you, and to lead you into biblical truth. I like to think of the salvation experience as getting a second chance in life. I am thankful that God does not give up on us as easily as we give up on ourselves. I was in need of more than a second chance. I needed a third and a fourth chance and God mercifully gave me those extended chances. If you have tried to live the Christian life and failed, do not give up no matter how hopeless your life may seem. God is a God of second, third, fourth and beyond chances. With Christ a new lease on life is just a twinkle of the eye away.

Biblical Communication: Speaking the Truth In Love

When we claim to be Christians, and our speech does not line up with that claim it turns people away from Christianity. I believe such a poor witness hurts the gospel message more than all the naysayers negative comments put together. This chapter is about developing and keeping healthy Christian relationships, and one way we do that is to communicate with others in a biblical way. The beginning point for all productive relationships is to speak the truth in love, "But, speaking the truth in love, may grow up in all things into Him who is the head—Christ" (Ephesians 4:15). When we talk with others, it is important for them to know that we are speaking to them in the spirit of Christ's love. Human love is so superficial in many aspects. In today's culture, the word love is thrown around like and old catcher's mitt. Mostly, it seems, in today's culture, we use the word love when we want something from someone else. In reality love is giving not taking. The kind of love we must show others is what the Scriptures call agape love.

Maxim Number One: Speak the Truth in Love

The great apostle Paul, stunningly, described agape love in 1 Corinthians 13: 4--7,

> Love suffers long *and* is kind; love does not envy; love does not parade itself, is not puffed up; does not behave rudely, does not seek its own, is not

provoked, thinks no evil; does not rejoice in iniquity, but rejoices in the truth; bears all things, believes all things, hopes all things, endures all things (italics theirs).

Love is a vital part of the human and Christian experience, but just expressing the word love towards others does not impress God, but what impresses God is how we demonstrate that love--especially to those folks who are hard to love. Do you know some folks in your life that are hard to love? Well, maybe there is, but we have to love them anyway.

Christ showed his love for the unlovable when he died for a bunch of ungrateful, sinful people. Accepting Jesus' sacrificial love is the best and most important decision you will ever make. The alternative is not very pleasant: trying to find completeness in this world apart from knowing the love of Jesus. Without knowing Jesus and understanding of the Scriptures; eventually, this world will leave you hollow, constantly seeking answers, but never able to discover them.

There are many evil forces in the world trying to keep people from the truth of the gospel of Christ. According to the Scriptures, the blackness of the lower parts of the earth are eagerly awaiting for those who refuse Christ's invitation to be saved from such a horrible place, "Hell from beneath is excited about you, to meet you at your coming; it stirs up the dead for you, all the chief ones of the earth; it has raised up from their thrones all the kings of the nations" (Isaiah 14:9). Satan and his little demons are eagerly waiting to welcome you to their torture chamber. Waiting, enthusiastically, to throw a party upon your arrival, but when the party's over there will be only torment and pain--which will last for all eternity. When your life on earth is over, without Christ, what follows is an eternity in torment and total darkness.

There is another party waiting for you in heaven when you turn from your sins to Jesus, "Likewise, I say to you, there is joy in the presence of the angels of God over one sinner who repents" (Luke 15:10). I know which party I want to be invited to. How about you? You can spend an eternity full of torment and pain. Or you can spend an eternity of peace and joy where there will be no more sorrow, pain, or tears. You have free will to choose. Choose Christ.

Have you ever experienced sacrificial love from someone you did not know? How did you feel after that experience? Have you ever showed that type of sacrificial love to a stranger? How did you feel afterwards? I bet you felt so good inside. You know Jesus felt good knowing that his death would bring millions of people from all nations to join him in heaven to worship God forever (cf. Hebrews 12:2). Jesus said, "There is no greater love than to lay down one's life for his friends (cf. John 15:13).

Agape Love is Long-suffering

The first principle of agape love is that it is long-suffering—meaning, "patient." Long-suffering refers to a quality that suffers wrong and does not seek revenge after being wronged, but shows the grace to forgive those who have hurt them time after time. We are commanded in the Scriptures to forgive others seventy times seven (cf. Matthew 18:22). That quality and quantity of forgives manifests God's forgiving character to the world because he forgives us again and again.

Children are God's most precious gift. And parents understand the seventy times seven mandate when it comes to forgiving their children. They continue to love and forgive them in spite of their flaws. Parents will sacrifice everything to give their kids a life free of pain; even though we cannot protect them from all the pain this world has to offer. But the best thing we can do to protect them is to speak the truth in love. Making them feel loved and safe at home prepares them for the challenges that will surely come their way. And teaches them the importance of saying no to the destructive pitfalls they will face in today's culture: drugs, alcohol, smoking, vaping, sexual immorality and more. Teaching children character traits that are truly important in life, and demonstrating those character traits for them to witness is the best protection you can offer them. When children are young, they want to be like their parents, so teach them and demonstrate to them the truly important things in life: faith in God, love of family, truth, integrity, faithfulness, honesty, and the importance of being a truly good person contributing to the welfare of others. I believe that a parent's love for their child is the closet kind of love that compares with God's love for you and me.

Agape Love is Kind

The Second principle of agape love is that agape love is kind: meaning, "gracious, benevolent, and pleasant." Kind, kindness, what powerful words they are. I think about how kind Jesus was to those he encountered, especially those who were tormented and hurting. Some were possessed by demons. Several had illnesses. Many were sorrowful and without hope. Many of the apostles struggled with life just as we do; some had given up on ever finding answers to the suffering and pain of life and in the process lost hope of ever realizing the coming Messiah—their promised savior. They must have felt spiritually abandoned as they waited and waited for Christ's appearance. It must have been a surreal experience to the future apostles, who were there when John the Baptist saw Jesus of Nazareth walking toward the Jordon River to be baptized, as they heard John cry out, "Behold! The Lamb of God who takes away the sin of the world!" (John 1:29).

Have you been waiting to meet the savior of the world? His name is Jesus Christ and he has been waiting to meet you too. The kindness Jesus showed to those who were afflicted touches my heart every time I read the four gospels. There is one such story in the Gospel of Mark that causes my eyes to get a misty glow. It is the story about a man who lived in the tombs and was possessed by many evil spirits.

This anguished man met Jesus one day and his whole life changed in an instant. Before meeting Christ, this man was living in the rock tombs (burial grounds) naked, crying out night and day and cutting himself. When the people tried to chain him, he simply broke the chains. The day Jesus arrived this demon possessed man ran to the shore to meet him. As Jesus stepped out of the boat, this broken man stumbled as he ran and fell at the feet of Jesus. I wonder what thoughts were flowing through that man's mind when Jesus asked the demons that possessed him all those years--how many are you? Suddenly, confronted by the radiance of Christ this fragile human being must have trembled when he heard himself answer, "We are legion." Jesus immediately rebuked those pesky demons casting them into a herd of swine; while the evil force possessing them sent them tumbling over a cliff into the water below.

The Bible tells us that this man, who was insane, is now sitting at Jesus' feet clothed and in his right mind. When he asked Jesus if he could come with him, Jesus answered, "Go home to your friends, and tell them what great things the Lord has done for you, and how He has had compassion on you" (Mark 5:19). I can visualize in my mind's eye, Jesus, beholding this poor tormented soul, who he had just set free, as he gazed upon him with such love and kindness in his eyes. When the day finally comes, and we look upon the face of Christ we will see such beauty, grace, and kindness that we too will fall at his feet, in awe, and worship him.

Some may think the miracle in this story is the destroying and casting out of the many demons. But I believe the real miracle of this story is the changed life of this man; who is now sitting at the feet of Jesus clothed and in his right mind. Jesus did not come to earth to cast out demons, which he did, but his mission was to change broken lives into whole lives. And he does that so well, if you will let him.

Another story that touches my heart and shows the kindness of our Lord Jesus is told in three of the four gospels: Matthew 9:20, Mark 5:25, and Luke 8:43. It is the story of an elderly woman who had been suffering from internal bleeding for twelve years. She had spent all her money on physicians, hoping to be healed, but she never got any better--only broker. One day this broken woman heard that Jesus was coming to town and she thought to herself, "If I can just touch his garment, I will be healed" (great faith: life transforming faith).

Jesus is in town! Now is the moment for action. (Christian faith often requires some kind of action.) She drops everything and heads to town. When she arrives, the crowds are pushing and shoving to get closer to Jesus. Some had fallen and were being stepped on. More determined than ever she fights through the thick, maddening crowd where all were battling to just get a glimpse of Jesus. Minds and hearts wondered. "Are the things they have heard about this man true?" "Is he the Messiah?" This weakened, frail woman, from years of blood loss, squeezes through the last obstacle to touch Jesus. There he is, "she hears herself scream!" Mustering all the strength and faith she has left she reaches toward Christ and touches the hem of his coat and miraculously she is healed that very second. Jesus stops--turns around—and looks at the woman! The elderly lady thinks she's in big trouble when Jesus says, "Who touched me?" Turning back towards Jesus she instantly falls at his feet (sound familiar) and confesses; "It was I who touched you Lord." In his kind way, and with his eyes full of love for her, he says, "Daughter, be of good cheer; your faith has made you well. Go in peace" (Luke 8:48). Some might believe that the storyline in this story is that Christ can heal. But I believe the real storyline is that you can come to Christ for physical, spiritual, and emotional healing and he will not judge you nor will he turn you away.

Agape Love Does Not Envy

The third principle Paul tells us about agape love is that it does not envy. Christ-like love is not envious of what others have; it does not jealously desire things it does not possess, nor does it sin to acquire those things from their rightful owner. We have all looked at what someone else possesses: money, career, house, car, and even a spouse and have felt envious of those things. But agape love rejoices with them and wishes them well. Agape love allows us to be content with the things we have, "Not that I speak in regard to need, for I have learned in whatever state I am, to be content" (Philippians 4:11).

It has been said that the one with the most toys at the end of their life--wins. I do not agree with that. What a childish thing to believe. The apostle Paul wrote in 1 Corinthians 13:11, "When I was a child, I spoke as a child; I understood as a child, I thought as a child; but when I became a man, I put away childish things." Isn't it time that we as a people and a nation put away childish things? The truth is, as the Bible teaches, you brought nothing into this world and you can take nothing out; but your soul. The destination of your soul does not depend on how many toys someone possesses at the end of their life, but depends on having faith in Christ.

Agape Love is not puffed up, nor is it Arrogant

The fourth principle of agape love is that it does not promote itself; is not puffed-up or prideful. Philippians 2:3 says, "In humility consider others as more important than yourselves." In contrast to the instruction of the Scriptures, how often do we put ourselves above everyone else; probably, most of the time? What if Jesus had put himself above everyone else and refused to go to the cross? It was within his power to do so. Jesus made it clear that he freely chose to give his life, "No one takes it from Me, but I lay it down of Myself. I have power to lay it down, and I have power to take it again. This command I have received from My Father" (John 10:18). He had God's permission to escape the horrors of the cross. In spite of every human emotion telling him not to go, Jesus fulfilled his Father's will and went to the cross. If Jesus had refused to put others above his own life we would all still be lost in our sins with no hope of redemption. Every one of us would have in his or her custody a stamped one-way ticket to the lower parts of the earth.

One of the things God hates is a prideful, haughty person and there is enough of that going on in our society today. Being humble, is such times as these, is a radical act. God resists the proud and lifts up the humble. Be the kind of humble person that God can lift up; let him be the one who brags about you.

Agape Love does not Behave Rudely

The fifth principle of agape love is that it does not behave rudely." In today's society, it seems that being rude and difficult is kind of a badge of honor. Most of the reality T.V. shows I have seen consist of people being argumentative, hateful, and demanding their own way. No wonder our world is falling into a gorge of despair and uncertainty. I see the world slipping and sliding, trying to get traction, but going nowhere. Self-righteous people drowning in a landslide of hateful confrontation are a formula for disaster. What makes people believe they have the right to harm others for their own self-proclaimed beliefs and social status? I often wonder what God thinks as he looks down on the world we live in. If the heart of mankind does not change how long will God continue to be patient with us?

I have faith the circumstances in America and around the world could change. I believe that love is more powerful than hate; forgiveness is more powerful than not forgiving, understanding and knowledge is more powerful than prejudice and ignorance, kindness is more powerful than meanness, giving is more powerful than taking, and truth is more powerful than lies. Call me naïve for hoping these things will prevail in my lifetime. But they must, or the world will destroy itself. Soon the people of the world are going to see through the facade of those leading the nations and put an end to this madness, insisting on integrity and godly attributes within the leadership of governments.

Agape Love does not seek its Own Things

The sixth thing on Paul's list is that Agape love does not seek its own things. Agape love does not seek out ways to make personal gain but seeks the things that are Christ's; Philippians 2:21, "For all seek their own, not the things which are of Christ Jesus." The world has become a place of taking not of giving. You can only take so long because soon there will be nothing left to take, including positive human relationships.

Always taking, never giving back destroys everything that is good. Many large corporations and ministries have fallen apart because of greed, sexual immorality, and power struggles? Power struggles bring out the very worst in people: it is all about me; I must be in control. Righteousness never blossoms out of selfish people seeking their own way, especially when seeking wealth and power. Sinful behavior in any form is destructive. The damage might not be visible in the beginning, but sin, when acted upon, always catches up with you and it always destroys. Sinful behaviors can never build-up a person, a marriage, a nation, a family, or a company. Sin always tears down.

Agape Love is not Easily Provoked

The seventh thing about Agape love is that it is not easily provoked. Agape love is not easily made angry and it does not retaliate. Jesus, after being hit by an officer of the Chief Priest and later by the Roman soldiers did not retaliate. In one case, Jesus, simply said' "If I have spoken evil, bear witness of the evil; but if well, why do you strike me?" (John 18:23). After spitting on Jesus, Roman solders, after placing a crown of thrones on his head, struck him repeatedly with a stick as his blood ran down his face (cf. Matthew 27:30). He humbly accepted every blow, without a word, knowing he was taking the strips due us, "He was wounded for our transgressions, "He was bruised for our iniquities. The chastisement for our peace was upon Him, and by His stripes we are healed" (Isaiah 53:5). We owe Jesus so much! No sacrifice for him is too much!

We should pray for Christ-like self-control. With that kind of restraint, think of how many foolish arguments could have been avoided. Not to mention the marriages that might have been mended, the many relationships healed, and the many wars that could have been avoided. When mankind separates itself from God's principles, it's charting a path to annihilation, "Before destruction the heart of a man is haughty, and before honor *is* humility" (Proverbs 18:12, italics theirs). "But those who desire to be rich fall into temptation and a snare, and *into* many foolish and harmful lusts which drown men in destruction and perdition" (1 Timothy 6:9, italics theirs).

Agape Love Thinks no Evil

The eighth principle of agape love is that it thinks no evil. Agape love believes the best about people and sees the best in them. That is hard to do as we look around the world today. There is so much anger spilling over in the hearts of men and women in today's societies. That makes it difficult to visualize the best of humankind when we see so much hatred around us. But we must try, because Jesus saw enough "*good*" in the human heart to give his life to save mankind from destruction.

In order to see the good through the bad, we must possess Christ-like love in the depth of our hearts. What did Jesus proclaim from the cross right before he died? "Forgive them because they know not what they do" (Luke 23:34). Were those evil men that crucified and beat Jesus? Yes, but Jesus still saw the good in them. I wonder how many of those people in attendance that day became Believers, because they heard Christ's forgiving words. They witnessed perfect love from someone they rejoiced over killing. Are there people in your life you need to forgive? Forgive those people and see how quickly God rewards your obedience.

Agape love overlooks wrongs and finds ways to love the unlovable. It is not enough to love those who love you. Jesus confronts that type of one sided love in Luke 6:32, "But if you love those who love you, what credit is that to you? Even sinners love those who love them." Paul summarizes agape love in verse 7, "Love bears all things, believes all things and endures all things. Love never fails" (1 Corinthians 13: 6, 7,8a).

It is easy to write or talk about what agape love is but the difficulty comes in truly modeling that kind of love in every aspect of a Christian's life. I hope I have not left the impression that I have this agape love mastered because I certainly do not. My hope is that as I grow in my walk with Christ that this type of love will prevail more than the sinful qualities that so easily control the heart and human actions. We need to be aware of the type of love that is required from us as followers of Christ. So that we can keep striving toward that goal of loving like Christ loves.

I believe what Paul is trying to make very clear in these verses is the paradigm of how God loves each one of us. God's love is a perfect love and in order for Christians to find completeness in loving like God loves we will have to put-off our sinfulness and put-on Christlikeness, which is the Christians most challenging endeavor. Our sinful flesh will not release its control on the body willingly. This can only be accomplished by consistent spiritual warfare: walking in the Spirit not in the flesh (cf. Ephesians 6:10--18, Romans chapters 8, 9, 10). Loving like Jesus loves might seem impossible, but I believe with God all things are possible. Whether you have accepted Christ as savior or not, God still loves you perfectly and passionately and bids you to come to him as a dearly beloved child.

If you desire to go deeper, I have made a list of attributes that agape love is not, does not and what agape love is. Examine this list and honestly evaluate where you are in each one of these areas and make a plan for how you can better develop and model this type of sacrificial love to others. Read Ephesians 6:10-18, putting on the whole armor of God and Romans chapters 8, 9, 10, walking in the Spirit not in the flesh.

Agape love is not:
1. Envious
2. Easily provoked

Agape love does not:
1. Promote its self
2. Behave rudely
3. Seek own glory
4. Does not keep a record of wrongs

Agape love is:
1. Long-suffering
2. Kind

Maxim Number Two: Be Honest:

There is more to speaking the truth while communicating than not lying. How many of you while communicating with someone made yourself look better than you really deserved? Or how many of you have beaten around the bush during a conversation not really telling the other person what was on your mind or what really is bothering you. We cannot solve problems unless they are brought into the light and explained honestly and completely. Sometimes the truth hurts, but it is always going to eventually come to the surface. What is said in the closet will be made known. The truth always hurts more when found out instead of being expressed in love through honest communication.

It may seem redundant, but we must remove all dishonesty from our communications before we can build a relationship on trust. Trust is the basis for all good relationships. There are many pitfalls we can fall into when communicating with others. I think one of the worst is being afraid to speak the truth because it may hurt the other person or it may hurt you. But in the long run it is kinder to tell the truth from the beginning.

In order to speak the truth in love, there are several well entrenched bad habits we must put-off (cf. Ephesians 4:22-24). The first thing to put-off is outright deceit (lying). All of us have lied, and we knew we were lying. It is crucial in biblical communication to put-off lying and put-on truth. Secondly, guard against discrepancies in body language, tone of voice, and the selection of words. Nonverbal language speaks volumes to the one you are communicating with. Are the words you are speaking lining up with the actions of what your body is saying? Not only is it important to speak the truth in love we must also *model* the truth in love. Do not tell someone you love and forgive them with a distasteful look on your face. They will know you lack sincerity. Thirdly, do not fill your speech with innuendoes which includes denial, not taking responsibility for the issues at hand or blaming someone else for the situation. Blaming someone else is defined as, "blame shifting." Adam, the first man, was also the first blame shifter. When God confronted Adam about his sin, Adam immediately blamed it on Eve--sound familiar, "And God said, "Who told you that you *were* naked? Have you eaten from the tree of which I commanded you that you should not eat?" Then the man said, "The woman whom **"You gave to be *with me,"*** she gave me of the tree, and I ate" (Genesis 3:11, 12, italics theirs, bold emphasis mine).

Adam, trying to keep from taking responsibility for his sin; actually, blamed his sinful behavior on God, "The woman You gave me." Are you blaming God for your sinful behavior? Enabling you to deny you are the problem? We must be honest with ourselves and take responsibility for our own sinful actions. Blame shifting did not work for Adam and it will not work for you. God knows the truth. In biblical communication, you must take responsibility for your part in the situation, whether good or bad.

Let's review the rules spelled out in this maxim.

- First, we put-on honesty: being honest with yourself and others. It is a sin to lie to God, others, and foolishness to lie to yourself.
- Secondly, you must admit your fault in the situation: taking responsibility for your own actions.
- Thirdly, be sincere in your repentance and reconciliation. When you have done wrong, admit it and seek reconciliation quickly.

Maxim Number Three: Keep Current:

"Be angry but do not sin do not let the sun go down on your anger, nor give place to the devil" (Ephesians 4:26, 27). Holding on to anger is destructive to any relationship. That action throws open the door for Satan, allowing him a foothold in the relationship. Once he squirms his way in, he will wreak havoc into the relationship causing even more problems. When you harbor unrighteous anger, it begins to build and build and if it hangs around long enough--it will explode. The only reasonable solution to this dilemma is to resolve the issue as soon as possible through honest communication, repentance, and forgiveness.

Not all anger is sinful, as Jesus demonstrated when he tossed over the tables in the temple; because of the selling of merchandise in the house of God (cf. Matthew 21:12, Mark 11:15, John 2:15). What makes anger sinful? Answer, the motivation behind that anger. Anger becomes sinful when it is used to attack yourself or others. Failure to resolve anger when it occurs creates negative and sinful behavior and opens the way to disappointments, resentments, bitterness, and even hatred (malice). Unresolved anger will destroy all relationships. It will quickly put an end to the most important of human relationships: your marriage, your relationship with your children, your relationship with other family members, friends and coworkers. Ask yourself this question. Do problems escalate when they remain unresolved? The answer has to be yes. The longer you let unresolved issues go the harder they become to resolve. Past circumstances get distorted in time because the facts get lost and it makes it much harder to sort it all out and get to the core of the anger.

Anger becomes sinful when you clam up--also known as the silent treatment. When you refuse to talk, you cut off communication by refusing to discuss the issues. The different ways of clamming up consist of crying, working on someone's sympathy, distorting the true issues by dancing around the truth; threatening to throw a fit in order to avoid the unpleasantness of talking about why you are angry, and bottom lining. (Like Forest Gump would say, "That's all I got to say about that.)" Walking out in the middle or any part of the discussion and refusing to deal with the issues at hand has never solved anything. But instead causes more problems.

Deal with problems quickly before they have a chance to simmer and grow. Communicating biblically means we quickly resolve the issues that are at the core of the anger. It is foolishness to carry distresses over to tomorrow. There will be enough worry to deal with when the next day rolls around. Trouble + trouble = trouble. Despair does not take long to add up and unresolved issues do not just go away; instead, they multiply if left unsettled. What was once a "mole hill" will become a mountain!

Before entering into a situation to resolve an issue, ask yourself these five questions:

- Do I have all the facts straight? "He who answers a matter before he hears it, it is folly to him" (Proverbs 18:13).
- Is it sinful? Should love hide it? Is it hindering growth? Discern whether or not it would be better to forgive the person and move on--is it worth a confrontation? 1 Peter 4:8, "And above all things have fervent love for one another, for love will cover a multitude of sin."
- Is my timing right? Make sure it is the right time to talk to someone about the issue. Do not try to talk with someone when they are overwhelmed with something else, "And a word spoken in due season, how good it is" (Proverbs 15:23b).
- Is my attitude right? Am I trying to help the other person? Am I prayed up? Am I ready to speak the truth in love? But speaking the truth in love, may grow up in all things into Him who is the head—Christ" (Ephesians 4:15).
- Have I asked for God's help in prayer? "Trust in the Lord with all your heart, and lean not on your own understanding" (Proverbs 3:5).

It seems a lot of people in today's society think if you throw in a few threatening cuss words during a heated conversation you will intimidate or frighten someone into doing what you want. That is not what Scripture teaches, "Let no corrupt word proceed out of your mouth, but what is good for necessary edification that it may impart grace to the hearer" (Ephesians 4:29).

God's Word teaches that we are to separate ourselves from the world. When you communicate with someone, can they tell by how you communicate that it is different from the way the world communicates? Is there truth and love in your communication? Do you speak in a way that edifies the other person? Is what you are saying in agreement with your body language?

Maxim Number Four: Attack Problems Not People

Avoid words that attack a person's character by calling them hurtful names or making fun of them. That type of communication is so unhealthy because it further damages the relationship. Stay away from words that attack others, tear down relationships, and hinder spiritual growth. An unkind word will grieve the Holy Spirit; and when it comes to getting to the truth and reconciling a relationship, for a Christian, the key person in that process is the Holy Spirit. Let Him lead the conversation and you will be amazed how quickly problems can be resolved. By using words that edify, encourage, and lift up the other person. When using biblical principles of communication, you will succeed where you have failed in the past. Give it a try.

Our natural tendency is to react sinfully when attacked verbally. Reacting to situations in a sinful way should not be an option for a Christ-follower. Instead of reacting in a sinful way, we must learn to put-off our sinful nature and put-on Christ-likeness. I am a firm believer that when you put-off something bad--sinful nature--you must put-on something good--Christ-likeness--in its place, or you will return to the same old destructive habits you struggled with in the past.

Jesus is our example and when he was accused and verbally attacked he did not rage about his innocence. Although he was innocent,

For to this you were called, because Christ also suffered for us, leaving us an example, that you should follow His steps: *"Who committed no sin, Nor was deceit found in His mouth"*; who, when He was reviled, did not revile in return; when He suffered, He did not threaten, but committed *Himself* to Him who judges righteously" (1 Peter 2:21-23, italics theirs).

Through the indwelling of God's Spirit, we can learn to be kind, tenderhearted, and forgiving in the most uncomfortable situations. Because we have the confidence that Christ is guiding us. And he has promised to work all things out for our good. We can learn to communicate in a biblical way no matter what the situation might be. The really neat thing is that when the Holy Spirit begins to manifest the Gift of the Spirit in your life biblical communication will naturally flow out of you. Putting-off bad habits is not easy but it can be done by completely surrendering to the work of the Holy Spirit. (cf. 1 Cor. 10:13, Phil. 4:13). Keep in mind, when communicating, no matter how irrational or foolish the other person becomes you must act and speak biblically.

Why does the Bible have so much to say about how we should communicate? Why is that so important? According to James, in order to become a perfect (spiritually mature) man or woman you must learn to control your tongue, "For we all stumble in many things. If anyone does not stumble in word he is a perfect man, able also to bridle the whole body" (James 3:2). Who is the only man to have accomplished that perfection? Jesus! We must, to the best of our ability, develop Christ-like communication skills.

There is so much significance in words that the whole earth was created by the spoken Word of God (cf. Genesis 1:3). Words can build up or they can tear down. What if God had said "Let the darkness prevail;" instead of saying, "Let there be light?" Where would we be? Words are like a bullet fired from a gun; once you pull the trigger on those words and they have left your mouth, whether good or bad, they cannot be brought back. Words have the ability to cut deeper than any knife. James says that once hateful words leave the mouth they set on fire the course of nature and that fire is fanned by hell fire (cf. James 3:6) . Why is it important to speak in a way that is loving, kind, edifying, and forgiving? As Christ's representatives we are called to show the love of Christ to a hurting and lost world. Manifesting Christ's love to others identifies us as God's children. The command to love others was given so those who do not know Jesus can meet him through us, "Love one another so the whole world will know that you are My disciples" (John 13:35). Being like Christ, starts with the ability to control our tongue. Jesus is our example and he is the greatest communicator that has ever lived. And the more like him we become; the better communicators we will turn out to be.

Maxim Number Five: Be a Good Listener

When having a conversation with someone, there is always the tendency to interrupt them before they are finished talking. Most of us just cannot wait to give them our take on the situation. I do not believe in most instances this is intentional. But there is a fear of forgetting what intellectual advice you have stored up in life's experiences. But this is a mistake when trying to resolve an issue. When you interrupt the person that is talking, it gives them a chance to rethink something they were ready to say which might have gone a long way in resolving the issue. Let them finish. Then you can speak what is on your mind. When I was counseling, I would make a note of a comment or a Scripture the Lord put on my mind so I would not forget it. If you must interrupt, make it as short as possible. James in his epistle wrote, "So then, my beloved brethren, let every man be swift to hear, slow to speak, slow to wrath" (James 1:19). That is great advice but hard to do: to listen more than you speak. Steven R. Covey in his book, *The 7 Habits of Highly Effective People*, said this about being a good listener, "To relate effectively...we must learn to listen. And that requires emotional strength. Listening involves patience, openness, and the desire to understand." Those same qualities are outlined in the Scriptures, as well, for a Christian to develop while communicating.

When needing to keep my mouth shut, I use the image of riding a motorcycle or a riding lawn mower to remind me of the importance of keeping my mouth closed. Unless you like the sting and taste of bugs in your mouth you quickly learn to put a zipper on your lips. Whenever tempted to interrupt someone, when their speaking, I think about how untasteful it is to swallow a large June bug.

We can all get better at communicating biblically. I want to encourage you to practice the five maxims of biblical communication. I made a list of principles that when put into action, I believe, will help you be a better biblical communicator:

- Be a good listener: Listen more than you speak.
- Be specific: Communicate your feelings clearly.
- Speak as if Christ is speaking in all your communications.
- If you don't understand something said ask for clarification.
- Tell them to feel free to ask for clarification from you.
- Pray for God's guidance: invite the Holy Spirit into the conversation.

I hope this Chapter has helped you to better understand how to communicate based on biblical communication principles. If you desire to go deeper, read Ephesians 4:25-32 and make a list of areas in your biblical communication skills where you need to improve. And put together a plan of action to work on those areas.

Chapter 11

My Life after Christ

In the first few chapters of this book, I wrote about how far from God I had slipped, and the depravity which swept over me like a tidal wave pouring over the shore. At times my life seemed so hopeless. I *felt* I would never be free of my addictions. I often wondered, while observing others living their lives free from alcohol or drug abuse why was I so different? Why did I drink until I was unable to even stand? Why couldn't I have a couple of beers and be done? It seemed hopeless I would ever be free from addiction and all the pain and ugliness that goes with it. But God met me exactly where I was. As soon as I committed completely to him, he began to change my life. I am not sharing what God has done in my life to draw attention to anything I have accomplished, but to assure you that God can use anyone no matter how far they might have slipped away from him. The Lord is willing and able to give you a life of meaning and purpose--which was so lacking in my own life.

The shame and guilt I felt over the sins I committed weighted me down like a fifty-pound rock clinging to my neck. It seemed impossible that I would ever be able to get unfettered from those destructive feelings. I was sure when Jesus looked down at me he saw a body so black and stained by sin it was unredeemable. I *felt* that in his sight I must look like a piece of coal buried deep in the earth destined to never see the light of day. I want to share another poem with you to describe how I *felt* about my hopeless life before Jesus plucked me, suffocating, out of the depths of a miry sink hole.

Please forgive me for boring you with another poem, but this poem describes the hopelessness I *felt* about the state of my life and then the joy I found in a relationship with Jesus,

The color of my sin

Charcoal colored body of sin all
Covered in black because of my transgressions
Is how I looked to Him.
Punishment and torment is what I have earned.
All my sins, I've tried, but can't unlearn.
My sins covered me like blackened coal dust.
And every day I now cling to His mercy and learn to trust.
Forgive me my sins, Lord, don't leave me behind!
Christ has freed me from the chains that bind.
Sacrifice, blood, and water He gave.
Hallelujah! Christ rose from the grave.
Nothing could stop Him, for that was His Father's will.
He died to save mankind.
We are so ill.
Charcoal colored bodies of sin washed clean by His blood.
His grace and mercy now cover me like a flood.
Thanks for your grace; it's not what I deserved.
Punishment and death is what I reserved.
Jesus wouldn't have it; He said I will go;
To show how the Father's mercy and love, will flow.
Charcoal colored bodies of sin, washed clean by Him.
White raiment you have given to cover my sin.
Thank you Lord Jesus! I can live again!

Yes, thank you God for sending your Son to save mankind from destruction. It took a while, but I soon came to realize that God did not see me as a stained and worthless lump of flesh. Instead his eyes saw a lost sheep that needed a shepherd. As he looks at me now, his word assures me that he no longer sees my sin but sees the precious Blood of Christ which covers me. All those wasted years! At fifty years old, I finally understand that Christ is where my hope should have been all along. Do not waste any more precious time seeking the things of this world, but seek the things that are of God which do not rust, get stolen or rot.

My desire after giving my life to Christ was to help people with chemical addictions. God began to prepare me for ministry by getting me involved in a biblical counseling course. I completed that course of study and earned a certification in biblical counseling. I soon started counseling at my church. Shortly after I started counseling I got involved in a recovery ministry. Working in a recovery ministry I was no longer limited to counseling one or two persons at a time, nor was I limited to just one area of recovery. I began to become familiar with other destructive habits: co-dependency, sexual addiction, pornography, anger, pride, selfishness, a controlling spirit, and those are just a few of the destructive tools that Satan uses to keep us in chains.

The recovery experience was an eye opening experience, which enabled me to see other areas of my life that were just as damaging to my spiritual growth and my relationships as chemical dependency. Pray that the Lord Jesus Christ will open your eyes to any negative character traits that need thrown into the crucible fire. And look deep into your soul and listen for the Lord to speak to you about any areas that are holding you hostage. Be honest with yourself, and allow Christ the freedom to change those negative traits into strengths. That cleansing process may be painful at first. It is not easy looking inside our own hearts and seeing the ugly stuff we carry around with us. But the freedom that comes from getting rid of all that baggage is worth every agonizing truth Christ reveals to you.

My time spent working in a recovery ministry gave me an opportunity to teach to a large group of people--public speaking. I was so fearful of public speaking; when I had to do it, I would break out in a cold sweat, begin to shake, and would instantly freeze up. Public speaking had been my greatest fear as far back as grade school. Do not let your fears stop you from doing what God has put on your heart to do. His perfect love will overcome any fear you might have. Today as a pastor and ministry leader I speak to an audience regularly. Teaching, the Word of God, is my favorite thing to do. God will use what you fear the most and turn it into strength.

The Next Phase

After several years working in a counseling and recovery ministry, I felt the Lord calling me to another area of ministry. I did not have a clue as to what ministry he was calling me to at the time. I just knew it was time to step down from the other ministries and move on to new ground. God will always keep you moving forward in ministry, leading you into new areas that will stretch you and grow you spiritually. No one was more surprised than I was when God moved me into a pastorate. I was in my early sixties and starting a whole new adventure. God is good. And with him on your side no accomplishment will be impossible for you.

Long before getting involved in Christian ministry I worked at a factory. During my time there, since they would pay for it, I decided to get a college degree. Not an easy decision for someone who quit high school in the tenth grade (I did get my GED in the army). Originally I sought a degree so I could advance on my job. A few months later that factory closed and I was halfway through my degree program. Once they closed the doors, the company where I was working would no longer pay for my college courses. God is faithful and he supplied the rest of the finances through a retraining program. Through some ups and downs I earned a bachelor's degree in business administration. I did not realize it at the time but that degree was part of the Lord's plan for my future in ministry.

Let me talk for just a moment about God's plan for you. One

thing that was missing in my life, before Christ, was that I felt worthless. I had never accomplished anything worthwhile in my life and never figured I would. I *felt* that I had let everyone in my life down. My mind dulled by alcohol and drugs; I often asked myself-- why am I here? I saw no future for myself. But God had a wonderful plan for me and to realize that plan it took surrendering my life to Jesus and trusting God with my future. God has a perfect plan for each one of his children, including you. Christ has the ability to take a broken life and turn it into a life that sparkles for the entire world to witness. Get on board. Turn the helm of your life over to Christ, so you can realize the wonderful plan God has already set in motion for you; but you must reach out and seize it.

"BUT," there seems to always be a "but;" doesn't there? If you are not willing to practice the biblical disciplines required to grow in your Christian walk you will most likely never realize the complete and perfect plan God has for you. For each one of us, it is essential that we pursue and digest spiritual food in order to grow. We find that spiritual food in the Word of God,

> Jesus was led up by the Spirit into the wilderness to be tempted by the devil. And when He had fasted forty days and forty nights, afterward He was hungry. Now when the tempter came to Him, he said, "If You are the Son of God, command that these stones become bread. But He answered and said, "It is written, *'Man shall not live by bread alone, but by every word that proceeds from the mouth of God* (Matt. 4:1-4, italics theirs).

Jesus is crystal clear. There is food for the body and food for the soul, and which one should you desire the most? Food for the soul! In this biblical account, Satan uses the desire for food to tempt Jesus. Food and water are the strongest survival instincts of mankind. Without either one of them the body would wither and die. In order to put this biblical account in its correct context, we must remember that Jesus has not eaten or drank anything for forty days and nights. He is dehydrated and starving to death. While being tempted, even in his state of near death, Jesus uses the Word of God-- the true bread for life--to rebuke Satan--sending him on his way. We must learn to trust in God's Word while we are being tempted: using it as a weapon. The word of God is a two-edged sword cutting to pieces every lie Satan lobs at you; nothing will send the devil running for his life as fast as the Word of God.

Jesus taught his disciples that the Word of God produces life and health in our lives, "He who received seed on the good ground is he who hears the word and understands *it,* who indeed bears fruit and produces: some a hundredfold, some sixty, some thirty" (Matt. 13:23, italics theirs). We need spiritual food to remain spiritually healthy. I believe the first sign of a Christian's falling away is when he or she no longer has a desire to read the Bible. Having a steady diet of God's Word is essential for remaining spiritually healthy. It is a matter of life and breath for a healthy soul.

Do you have the same craving to nourish your spiritual body as you do your physical body? When you pick up a Bible to read do you feel excitement? Anticipating what insight, what revelation, and for what God is going to teach you from his word that day? God knows your heart and he knows if his word is falling on fertile soil or on the rocks. When we read study and meditate on God's word, we are ingesting the Bread of Life. Jesus said, "I am the living bread which came down from heaven. If anyone eats of this bread, he will live forever; and the bread that I shall give is My flesh, which I shall give for the life of the world" (John 6:51).

Jesus distinguishes the difference between earthly food for the body and spiritual food for the spirit. Earthly food sustains the body on earth until it dies. But the spiritual food Jesus is offering sustains the soul through this life and on through eternity. Jesus is "one" with us, by the indwelling of the Holy Spirit. He is the Bread of Life that sustains the Holy Spirit and keeps it alive. As we take in our daily spiritual food, we begin to grow in our understanding of who Jesus is and we begin to live out our commitment to him. With a healthy spiritual diet of God's Word, and prayer our daily walk with him will shine like a beacon on a hill.

I do not want to stumble or crawl into heaven. I want to cross that finish line full speed, with arms outstretched, ready to embrace Jesus and hear those legendary words, "Well done good and faithful servant." I believe you do too. So put as much emphasis, or, better yet, more emphasis, on feeding your spiritual body than your physical body: having a hunger heart for the life-giving Word of God.

After the plant where I worked closed, I went on unemployment while finishing my degree program. Soon the unemployment ran out. I really thought with my manufacturing experience and having a college degree I would have no trouble finding a job. But America was in a recession, and I was not able to find work. The road to being a pastor started here. I had been thinking about being a pastor for a while, but had no confirmation that was where God was leading me. After all I was doing pastoral work as a counselor and recovery leader. I thought to myself, "What does it take to be a pastor." So I asked a pastor friend that question. He said that I needed to hang around with him awhile so that is what I did. I accompanied him to churches where I shared my testimony. He schooled me on the finer points of being a pastor: he taught me how to prepare and deliver sermons, perform weddings, funerals, and the importance of making yourself available to your congregation--at all times.

After preaching at a few churches, one of those churches offered me the opportunity to be their pastor and I accepted. God started me on a marvelous journey which I am still on. I became a recorded minister of the gospel by the Indiana Yearly Meeting of the Religious Society of Friends, July 27, 2017. Being recorded as a minister of the Gospel of Christ, is a memory I will always cherish. I was able with the financial help of the Indiana Yearly Meeting and my church family to earn a Master's degree in Transformational Leadership-Spiritual Formation. Finally, the icing on the cake, I am a published

Christian author and I am now working on my second book. Praise God for all he has done for me!

I am amazed how far God has brought me and I am excited about what he has planned for me next. God took me from a drunkard wallowing in my own self-pity and blaming everyone else for my failures to a recorded minister of the gospel. Is there anything too hard for the Lord? "Behold, I *am* the LORD, the God of all flesh. Is there anything too hard for Me? (Jeremiah 32:27). No matter how hopeless you feel. No matter how gloomy the future looks. No matter how out of step you seem. God can turn those feelings of hopelessness into a symphony of beautiful music for you to dance to. All you need to do is give him permission to do it. Then do all you can to learn about this wonderful savior and begin building a relationship with him.

Chapter 12

Striving for Completeness in Love, Joy, and Peace

It is amazing what God can do to a willing heart that is totally committed to serving him. In the next few chapters, I want to discuss areas in our lives that I have come to understand are crucial for achieving spiritual maturity--completeness. The Christian life is all about putting on the character of Christ (spiritual formation) and the first three attributes of the Gift of the Spirit is love, joy and peace.

Striving For Completeness In Love

I know I have already written extensively on love in chapter ten. In that chapter, my intent was to demonstrate what sacrificial love looks like in the life of a follower of Jesus. Speaking about love in this chapter my hope is to explain how and where we need to demonstrate sacrificial love.

The word love is such a misused and misunderstood word in our society today that in order to help us to better understand the concept of sacrificial love; I believe it would be beneficial to talk about the three Greek words used in New Testament times for the word love. The first word on the list is Eros: "referring to erotic or sexual love." The word Eros was not used in the New Testament

Scriptures, but was commonly used in Greek literature at the time; so people understood its meaning. The second word used for love in New Testament times was the word Phileo, which refers to "tender affection towards a friend or relative." The third word used for love in the New Testament Scriptures is the word Agape, which we talked about extensively in chapter 10. The word agape was used by Believers to denote the unconditional, sacrificial love of God for his children.

The word love is tossed around in today's culture like a fix all for summing up human approval: I love that, I love those shoes, I love that show, I love this and I love that. The word love is not meant to explain what you are feeling about trivial things. Love is a deep, deep emotion given to us from God. Some people refer to a sexual encounter as making love. Can humans really make love; like they make a chocolate cake? Love is a strong word and should never be used lightly. Because God is love (cf. 1 John 4:16). If the word love describes who God is than love should have the same reference in which we reference the All-mighty. He is the creator of love and uses that word to describe the reason he sent Jesus to die on the cross (cf. John 3:16).

I believe the watering down of the word love is a major reason why so many marriages fail today. True love needs to grow and be nourished. Love is meant to be giving not taking, and it must originate from the one who created such a strong emotion—God himself. God gives us a natural love for him, for our parents, for our children, and for our own lives. The perfect love of God is the glue that holds marriages and families together--including God's family. Love is a crucial component in the survival of the human race. If God ever removes his love from the earth the earth with all its wickedness will, in time, self-destruct.

Loving God with all Your Heart

Have you ever pondered how powerful a three letter word can be? Such a tiny three letter word is "all" a petite word which means a gigantic commitment. The word all appears 5665 times in 4719 verses in the NKJV of the Bible – Blue letter Bible. Have you ever said, "I am giving this my all?" Or maybe after success or failure, you said, "I gave it my all?" What does giving your all mean to you? The significance of that three letter word was spelled out by the Lord Jesus. He was very candid when he gave his definition of "all" to the Scribes in Mark 12:30. After asking Jesus, which is the first commandment of all? Jesus answered, "And you shall love the LORD your God with **all your heart**, with **all your soul,** with **all your mind**, and with **all your strength**. This *is* the first commandment" (Mark 12:30, italics theirs, bold emphasis mine). Jesus personified the sincerest meaning of giving it your all when he suffered and died on the cross at Calvary. Christ truly gave his all for all. Matthew Henry in his commentary on Mark 12:30 said,

> The great commandment of all, which is indeed inclusive of all, is that of loving God with all our heart. Loving God with all our heart, will effectually take us off from, and arm us against, all those things that are rivals with him for the throne in our souls, and will engage us to everything by which he may be honored, and with which he will be pleased; and no commandment will be grievous where this principle commands, and has the ascendant.

Loving the Lord with all your heart gives him dominance over your heart. This allows him to break down the ramparts you have erected to stand against his authority.

How often do you tell Jesus that you love him? How often do you sit in his presence and feel his love flowing through you? Love is a two way street and needs to flow both ways in order to grow. How heartwarming is it when someone you love says, "I love you," especially for no reason at all? It will certainly warm you and bring a smile to your face. Christ gave his all to save sinners. And in return, forgiven sinners, such as you and I, must surrender all of our heart to Jesus and give him permission to transform a selfish, self-centered heart into a heart overflowing with love for God and for our fellow human beings.

God never commands us to do something without a reason. So why is it important that we love God with all of our heart? Because Loving God with all your heart protects, sustains, solidifies, and communicates to your soul that Christ is the savior of the world. Flooding your heart with love for God protects your heart from so much of the intrusive and worthless things this world has to offer. When you have no room in your heart for sinful desires, the renewing of your mind becomes a natural part of your character; erecting stop signs against anything that tries to exalt itself above Christ, "Casting down arguments and every high thing that exalts itself against the knowledge of God, bringing every thought into captivity to the obedience of Christ" (2 Corinthians 10:5). That is what loving God with all your heart does. It removes the undesirable idols of the heart that we accumulate through the years.

I love the story of Phillip and the Enoch in acts chapter eight. Phillip explains to the Enoch, while riding in his chariot, that Jesus is the Christ the savior of the whole world. After Phillip's explanation, the Enoch believes in Jesus for his salvation and asks Phillip, "What hinders me from being baptized? Phillip answers, "If you believe with all your heart, you may." And he answered and said, "I believe that Jesus Christ is the Son of God" (Acts 8:37). We need to believe in Christ with all of our hearts, especially in these troublesome times when there are so many unwholesome distractions warring against God for our affections. Salvation is birthed in the heart. And that leads to the next reason we need to love God with all of our heart.

Protecting Your Heart

Loving God with all your heart protects it from following after idols, "Keep your heart with all diligence, for out of it *spring* the issues of life" (Proverbs 4:23, italics theirs). The Scriptures teach that life flows from the heart and because of that the heart must be guarded at all times. How many of you have ever built an idol out of metal and overlaid it with gold, or erected a carved image made of wood and worshiped it? Probably none of us, but how many of us have erected an idol in the heart? What do you place ahead of the Lord Jesus in your heart: alcohol, drugs, sex, cigarettes, selfishness, pride, money, power, or people (a short list)? Learning to love the Lord more and more is what removes the idols that are already established in the heart and erects a bulwark to keep new idols from invading the heart. If Jesus dose not rule your heart, he does not rule you!

Before coming to Christ, our heart has already been exposed to many idols. Some we allow to play a titanic role in determining the kind of person we are. Anything we worship apart from Christ is an idol and will only work to the devils advantage. Those idols must be displaced and replaced with Christ's love. We should never forget how deceitful the human heart is and how easily it gets distracted. Remember Eve in the garden? The idol of her heart at the moment she took a big bite out of that fruit was I want to be like God. And Satan convinced her that was a possibility? She fell for Satan's lie. Do not be deceived. There is only room for one God in the human heart! And that God is the Lord Jesus.

Trusting God with all Your Heart

Finally, it is important to love God with all of your heart because you must trust Him with all your heart, "Trust in the LORD with **all** your heart, and lean not on your own understanding; in **all** your ways acknowledge Him, And He shall direct your paths"

(Prov. 3:5-6, bold emphasis mine). A heart that totally trusts in the Lord is a heart that is steadfast and true to him. Trusting God and watching him work in your life, time after time, inscribes on the heart a journal of love, "Let not mercy and truth forsake you; bind them around your neck, write them on the tablet of your heart" (Proverbs 3:3). Maintain a Christ love journal written on the heart of the wonderful things he has done for you. And call on those memories in times of trials and temptations looking to the love of Christ to give you strength to overcome.

Jesus made it clear that the heart is the front lines of our war against Satan and is the battlefield where the fight rages to control our sinful nature: to put-off the old man and to put-on the new man. Jesus while teaching His disciples said, "For out of the heart proceed evil thoughts, murders, adulteries, fornications, thefts, false witness, and blasphemies" (Matthew 15:19). Remember that what you allow to inner into the heart determines your actions and the kind of a person you are going to be. That old adage, "garbage in, garbage out" is so true. You can choose "garbage in, garbage out" or you can choose "Jesus in, Jesus out" God has given us free will to make that all-important decision. Make the right one. Jesus!

Christ's Love Living in the Heart of a Believer

In Matt. 22: 39 Jesus said, "The second greatest commandment was to love your neighbor as yourself." Jesus went on to say in Matthew 22: 40 that "On these two commandments hang all the law and the prophets." Why is that significant? Because Jesus came to fulfill the law and he did that by showing perfect love for God and others. It is important to love others as Christ did because Jesus commanded us to, "A new commandment I give to you, that you love one another; as I have loved you, that you also love one another. By this all will know that you are my disciples; if you have love for one another" (John 13:34).

People should be able to identify you as a Christian by the love you show to your fellow human beings. Do people you come in contact with recognize you as a Christian? If so, would what they see cause them to want to be a Christian? Or would it turn them away?

Jesus left heaven to live in poverty on earth. In doing that he gave up his status in heaven and his equality with God and put on human flesh (cf. John 1:14). How painful that must have been for him. He gave his "all" for us and we are expected to give our "all" for him. That includes our time, our resources, our energy, and even our lives. We are commanded to serve others and do it in a way that shows them the love of Christ. Christ's love and kindness is what attracted people to him 2000 years ago, and that is what will draw them to him today. It is Christ-like love, from God's people, that will draw folks back to the church.

Christ Love Manifested in our Daily Lives; Saying no to the Things of This World

We are to have the love of Christ manifested in our daily lives, while separating ourselves from the desires of the world. A Christian's love should not be focused on the things of this world but on the things of the world to come (heaven). That does not mean we are to give away all of our possessions and live in a cardboard box. It means that if the things of this world become more important to you than the things of God than it is time to examine yourself and get your priorities straight. The material things we have belong to God anyway because he created everything on earth and in the heavens, "Indeed heaven and the highest heavens belong to the LORD your God, *also* the earth with all that *is* in it" (Deuteronomy 10:14, italics theirs). The possessions we have are to be used to support ourselves, our families, and to expand God's kingdom on earth.

It is not a sin to have great riches. The sin comes when riches become an idol of the heart and are placed before God, which causes double-mindedness damaging your relationship with him, "Those who desire to be rich fall into temptation and a snare, and into many foolish and harmful lusts which drown men in destruction and perdition. For the love of money is a root of all kinds of evil, for which some have strayed from the faith in their greediness, and pierced themselves through with many sorrows" (1 Tim. 6:9, 10). Scripture is clear; it is the *love of money* that is the root of all evil. Not money itself. The most damaging thing about loving money is the damage it causes to your relationship with God: you begin to depend on money and things instead of depending on God.

God delights in blessing his children with material things; after all, in the beginning, he gave mankind the whole earth to frolic about in. Some of the Old Testament prophets were rich: Abraham, Jacob, Job, and David, but with their wealth they honored God and the poor with what they had been given. The Lord makes it a high priority to care for the poor and needy. Especially when it comes to helping widows and orphans (cf. James 1:27). Those who continued to make helping the destitute a priority continued to prosper. Just as many of the Old Testament prophets were poor: Samuel, Isaiah, Jeremiah, and Elijah, but through their poverty they also honored God. God uses all kinds of people and circumstances to get his work accomplished. One mistake we do not want to make is putting limits on what God is able to do with a person no matter what their status in life is.

God commands us not to love the things of this world not because he wants to punish us or make us suffer but to protect us, "And the cares of this world, the deceitfulness of riches, and the desires for other things entering in choke the word, and it becomes unfruitful" (Mark 4:19). Loving the things of this world will cause you to lose your focus on what is really important. The most important thing in a Christian's life is to love God first and love others secondly. Lusting after the things of this world will smother you and will begin a downward spiral where you will begin to transgress in your Christian walk and begin to grow spiritually weak. And that is exactly where Satan wants to keep you. When you become spiritually weak, you stop reading your Bible, you stop praying, and you stop going to church. That is when Satan will pounce on you like a lion pounces on a crippled, lost gazelle. Keep in mind that things are not going to bring fulfillment to your life. Things will create a false feeling of peace, only to let you down later. Things can never fill the emptiness in the human heart. Only a perfect God that loves you perfectly can fill that lonely feeling on a cold, dark, and scary night.

Satan tempted Jesus with the things of the world after he wandered in the wilderness for forty days and nights. The devil, speaking to Jesus, said, "All these *things* I will give You if You will fall down and worship me" (Matthew 4:9, italics mine). All these things can be an overpowering desire which draws you into a web of lies and deceit that will eventually lead you to destruction. Jesus quickly responded to Satan in verse 10, "Away with you, Satan! For it is written, *'You shall worship the LORD your God, and Him only you shall serve'*" (Italics theirs).

It is a dangerous practice to ponder on any temptation too long. The best practice is to instantly say no by using Scripture to reject such thoughts from your mind. That is why it is good to have a few choice Scriptures memorized when such instances arrive. Scripture memorization is not as difficult as many try to make it. Memorizing Scripture is a great way to exercise your mind--increasing cognitive capacity. Memorization is like anything else the more you practice it the easier it becomes. Early on in my Christian walk I would write down, on 3x5 cards, Scriptures and carry them with me, and whenever I would get a few minutes I would pull them out and practice memorizing them. Excuse my redundancy, but if you want to live a lively Christian life you are going to have to work hard at it. One thing I have learned is that nothing worthwhile comes easy and that includes a vibrant, growing in Christ-likeness--life. Work hard!

James describes the dangers of allowing sinful desires to hang around in the heart to long, "But each one is tempted when he is drawn away by his own desires and enticed. Then, when desire has conceived, it gives birth to sin; and sin, when it is full-grown, brings forth death" (James 1: 14, 15). If worldly desires are allowed to simmer in the heart they will soon grow into an ugly, painful boil, ready to burst onto the surface destroying your joy and leaving you weakened and open to the devils attack. Possessions can quickly turn into idols of the heart; as our sinful heart begins to believe that if I just had a better job, more money, a bigger house and car, or a better spouse. Then I would be happy. There is nothing in this world that can make a soul happy if their relationship with the creator of those things is not right.

We are to love sacrificially, guard our hearts from loving the things of this world, and we are to show Christ-like love to others. In order to do those things, it takes obedience to God's word. Being a doer of the word (cf. James 1:22) allows the Word of God to get to work changing us from the inside-out--perfecting his love in us. We are not talking about a watered down love. We are talking about God's love manifesting itself in us producing a nation of people worthy to be called sons and daughters of God. I know human love is real and in its own jurisdiction is so worthy to be shared with others. But human love, cannot, and will not, change the heart of mankind, because it is diminished by our sinful nature. Only Christ-like love in the heart of God's people can change the woeful state of the world around us.

What is the final outcome of filling our hearts with God's perfect love? It is oneness with Jesus, God, and the Holy Spirit, "Love has been perfected among us in this: that we may have boldness in the Day of Judgment; because as he is; so are we, in this world" (1 John 4:17). We are to be the hands and feet of Christ in the world allowing our heavenly light to shine like a beacon upon the highest mountain for the entire world to witness. That will only be accomplished when the world observes the manifestation of God's perfect love in his people. That heavenly light, called the church, may be flickering, but it has not gone out. I believe with all my heart that God is going to breath on the church giving it new life causing a gigantic light to shine brightly in the heavens drawing his people back to the church of Jesus Christ. And this time there will be no retreat. The church will triumph in its quest to bring people to Christ.

God's Love is the tendon that holds the world and all of Christianity together. And without the love of God there would be no life-altering force on the earth,

> "He is the image of the invisible God, the firstborn over all creation. For by Him all things were created that are in heaven and that are on earth, visible and invisible, whether thrones or dominions or principalities or powers. All things were created through Him and for Him. And He is before all things, and in Him all things consist" (Colossians 1: 15-17).

I believe the evil we see in the world today is only a dim flickering flame compared to the raging inferno that will come when Christ returns to remove his church. God's love for us caused him to sacrifice his son to save mankind. And it was God's love that kept Jesus on the cross. And the Love of God is what keeps the evilness of this world from spinning, even more, out of control.

Chapter 13

Striving for Completeness
in Prayer and Trust

In order to experience strong spiritual growth, it is necessary to develop a powerful prayer life. Prayer in its simplest form is simply talking to God one on one. Do not be intimidated by prayer. Jesus Christ is the finest listener that as ever walked on this earth and he still listens intently to his children today. "Do you trust God with your prayers? Do you make time alone in prayer with God a priority? Your prayer life is only as important as you make it and your Christian walk is only as important as you make it. Jerry Bridges in his book, *Trusting God even when it hurts* said this about prayer; "Prayer is the most tangible expression of trusting in God."

We pray because we are planting seeds of trust, and depending on God's power to live a victorious Christian life. Through prayer and communion with the Holy Spirit, we can build a strong personal relationship with Jesus. To accomplish such a relationship requires putting forth the effort and being committed to spending quality time with him in Bible study and prayer. It is very difficult, or near impossible, to build a relationship with someone without spending time with them. Human relationships are important and spending time with family and friends should be a priority. But how much more important is it to build a lifelong relationship with the One who created the world and everything in it. Intimately knowing God is the ultimate joy of life and should be the pursuit of each individual. The apostle Paul wrote in 1 Thessalonians 5:17, "Pray without ceasing" that is a strong statement about how important prayer is in developing spiritual maturity--completeness. Without a strong prayer life, you will struggle to put-off the old man and put-on the character of Christ.

Fervent Prayer

Prayer by the Old Testament profits was a key to everything they did. Abraham heard God speak to him and dropped everything, packed up his family and his possessions, and left for a country he knew not where. That is trust. The Psalms are filled with David's passionate prayers to God. Including prayers of repentance,

> Wash me thoroughly from my iniquity,
> And cleanse me from my sin. For I acknowledge my transgressions,
> And my sin *is* always before me. Against You, You only, have I sinned,
> And done *this* evil in Your sight—
> That You may be found just when You speak,
> *And* blameless when You judge (Ps. 51:2-4, italics theirs).

It is essential for us to be honest in our prayers: admitting our sinful nature and seeking God's forgiveness. When we go before the Lord in prayer, humbling ourselves prepares us to stand before him without guilt and shame—we have laid our cards on the table--no more perceived secrets. Confessing our sins each time we speak with God gives us the confidence to share with him our deepest thoughts and hopes; honestly laying at his feet our prayers, our supplications, our concerns, our fears, and gaining the authority to pray for those we love. The Holman Bible Dictionary says this about being clean when coming before God in prayer, "The writing prophets noted that genuine prayer calls for accompanying moral and social accountability. Isaiah's call reflected the intense cleansing and commitment involved in Prayer."

The Old Testament prophets understood that before entering into our heavenly Father's presence it was crucial to go before him in honesty, sincerity, and with a clean heart. Are there sins in your life you need to confess? Do it now! And then enter into the very presence of God with confidence.

Pray Before a Major Decision and in Times of Stress

In the New Testament, Jesus' teachings inspired us to pray fervently, taught us how and when to pray. We know that Jesus prayed at crucial moments in his ministry. At those times, he would seek out a quiet place and ask his Father what he wanted him to do, "Now it came to pass in those days that He went out to the mountain to pray, and continued all night in prayer to God, "And when it was day, He called His disciples to *Himself;* and from them He chose twelve whom He also named apostles" (Luke 6:12-13, italics theirs).

Jesus spent the whole night in the mountains praying before choosing his twelve disciples; I wonder what took so long. Was Jesus trying to confirm his Fathers choices concerning the twelfth disciple? "Judas Iscariot, are you sure he is to be one of my twelve?" Jesus might have asked. (Remember that prayer is a conversation between you and God.) It is ok to ask questions to make sure you understand exactly what God is saying to you. God will never punish you or laugh at you for asking for clarification. When in prayer, it is crucial to take the time necessary to listen for God to speak to you. I believe too many people believe that prayer is a one-way avenue of communication. But that is because many do not pause to listen for

God's still small voice. Be a good listener when communicating with the Lord. You might be surprised to hear what he has to say to you.

Jesus prayed in times of stress. Right before his arrest and crucifixion he took three of his disciples to the Garden of Gethsemane and prayed, "Then He said to them, "My soul is exceedingly sorrowful, even to death. Stay here and watch with Me" (Matt. 26:38). They fell asleep leaving Jesus to go off by himself as he prayed fervently for his Father to take away this bitter cup that had been placed before him, "Jesus went a little farther and fell on His face, and prayed, saying, "O My Father, if it is possible, let this cup pass from Me; nevertheless, not as I will, but as You *will*" (Matt. 26:39, italics theirs). Jesus did not want to suffer the pain and shame of the cross. But he knew that was the only solution to the, otherwise, incurable disease of sin that plagued mankind. Jesus did not want to die; after all, he was 100 percent man as well as being 100 percent God and man has a natural instinct to live. But he chose to do God's will--not his own.

Humbling ourselves while engaged in prayer with God allows us to accept his will for the situation. Often God does not answer our prayers the way we want him to but, like Jesus, we must accept God's decision. Be patient and wait upon the Lord's timing. Remember, perfect patience is working perfectly to make you perfect and complete, lacking nothing (cf. James 1:4).

The apostle Paul discovered that his will does not always line up with God's will. He asked the Lord Jesus three times to heal him of a thorn in his side, but Jesus refused (cf. 2 Cor. 12:8-9). Why? In Paul's case it was to keep Paul humble. That is not always the reason God does not answer our prayers the way we want him to, but I believe it is one of the main reasons. We are often self-seeking in our prayers. Asking God for what we think is best for us; instead, of seeking his will for the situation. What happens to a Christian ministry when the leader gets filled with pride? The ministry falls apart leaving broken people in its torrent. Jesus made sure that did not happen in Paul's ministry. The Lord had too much for Paul to accomplish than to allow him to get a swollen head. Paul learned that our petitions are sometimes denied by God in order to accomplish a greater good. Even Christ's prayer, in the Garden of Gethsemane, was denied by God for the greater good: for the redemption of lost souls.

Christ's Intercessory Prayer

Jesus taught us about intercessory prayer in John 17 when he interceded for his disciples and for those who would believe in him through their sharing of the good news,

> I pray for them. I do not pray for the world but for those whom You have given Me, for they are Yours. "I do not pray that You should take them out of the world, but that You should keep them from the evil one. "I do not pray for these alone, but also for those who will believe in Me through their word (John 17:9, 15, 20).

Jesus' intercessory prayer continues today as he stands on the right hand of God interceding for you and me. But in order to reap the benefits of Christ's intercessory prayer you need to be part of God's family. Why? Because when you put your faith in Christ the Holy Spirit comes to live inside of you. The Holy Spirit's presence paves the way for unhindered communication between you and Jesus about your physical and spiritual needs. And those needs are communicated to God the Father who sits on his throne in heaven, "And he who searches our hearts knows the mind of the Spirit, because the Spirit intercedes for God's people in accordance with the will of God" (Rom. 8:27). So often we do not know what is best for us. But the Spirit of God knows and intercedes on our behalf.

The Holy Spirit is the third person of the trinity. It is God talking to God about you and we do not even realize it is happening. The Three are making plans to fulfill God's will for your life! Amen.

Pretty amazing when you think about how intimately God is involved in your life. While this secret communication is going on, it is imperative to keep in mind that we can disconnect this Christian lifeline if we do things that are not pleasing to the Lord, "And do not grieve the Holy Spirit of God, by whom you were sealed for the day of redemption" (Ephesians 4:30.

What have we learned about prayer in this chapter?

- We need to be clean when we enter into the presence of God: standing before him with a repentant heart.
- We need to pray before important decisions and in stressful situations.
- When we pray, we are trusting in Christ to do what is best for us.
- God does not always answer our prayers the way we want him to but according to his will.
- Jesus prays to the Father for our protection: to protect us while we are in the world from the evil one.
- Jesus prays for those who will believe in him through our sharing of the good news.

How Not to Pray

Jesus cautioned us not to pray to impress others and not to pray vain repetitions,

> And when you pray, you shall not be like the hypocrites. For they love to pray standing in the synagogues and on the corners of the streets, that they may be seen by men. Assuredly, I say to you, they have their reward. "But you, when you pray, go into your room, and when you have shut your door, pray to your Father who *is* in the secret *place;*

and your Father who sees in secret will reward
you openly And when you pray, do not use vain
repetitions as the heathen *do*. For they think that
they will be heard for their many words (Matt. 6:5-
-7, italics theirs).

Have you ever been to a prayer meeting when someone went on
and on and you began to wonder "Are they ever going to stop?" After
a long repetitive prayer, you twitch a bit, and start to wonder how
sincere their prayer really is. You ask yourself, "Were they sincere,
or did they just want to receive praise for what a great prayer they
prayed?" Jesus' instructions for pray are to get alone in your prayer
closet and pray to him one on one. When we pray, we are requesting
that God do something for us or someone else. Our prayers are not
for someone else's entertainment or to boost our own ego. In Jesus'
warning about using vain repetitions in prayers, he is not telling us
not to be persistent in our prayers; but cautions us not to allow our
prayers to become insincere and without feeling.

Our prayer life must be energized by faith. Prayers without
faith are like speaking into a tape recorder that is turned off. It
just does not register. Do not pray prayers that you do not expect
God to answer. Spewing out fancy words as fast as you can in an
attempt to impress God is like that tape recorder. They fall on deaf
ears. John MacArthur in his commentary said this about repetitious
prayers, "Prayers are not to be merely recited, nor are our words to
be repeated thoughtlessly, or as if they were automatic formulas."

I believe what is missing in those types of prayers, and why
God rejects them, is the key ingredient to any sincere prayer--love.
We pray because we love God and want to have a conversation with
him to discuss life and seek his help. The Scriptures teach us to be
persistent in our prayers (cf. Luke 18:1-5). But not praying as you
are reciting a written script, but sincerely from the heart: coming
fervently, passionately, and humbly before the Lord.

As you look back at the Old Testament prophets, you can feel the fervent intensity in their prayers. They were pouring out their hearts to God. I think of Job as he sought answers to his situation: losing everything he had. David's passionate prayer of repentance after his sin with Bathsheba was found out. Jeremiah, the weeping prophet, when seeking answers for why the nation of Israel would not believe him. But rather chose to believe false prophets. In the New Testament, James wrote about the rewards of passionate, cleansing prayer, "Confess *your* trespasses to one another, and pray for one another, that you may be healed. The effective, fervent prayer of a righteous man avails much" (James 5:16, italics theirs). I do not think anything moves the heart of God like sincere, honest, and heart felt prayers that are filled with love for God and others.

The Lord's Prayer

Luke tells us that after Jesus prayed he was asked by his disciples to teach them to pray. Jesus responded, "When you pray say,"

> Our Father in heaven, Hallowed be Your name.
> Your kingdom come. Your will be done on earth
> as *it is* in heaven. Give us this day our daily bread.
> And forgive us our debts, as we forgive our debtors.
> And do not lead us into temptation, But deliver us
> from the evil one. For Yours is the kingdom and the
> power and the glory forever. Amen (Matt. 6:9-13,
> italics theirs).

When we go before the Lord in prayer, the first thing Jesus tells us to do is to give honor to our Heavenly Father's name. I believe we do this through adoration, praise, and worship; humbly recognizing God for who he is and what he has done for us. Secondly, we are to pray for God's will to be done on earth and then accept his will. Thirdly, thanking God for our daily provisions. Fourthly, we thank him for forgiving our sins and giving us the strength to forgive others. Finally, seeking his protection against the evilness of this world and looking for direction in avoiding the temptations that so often over take us.

I believe prayer ranks as one of the highest priorities in a Believers life and at the same time is one of the most abused spiritual disciplines. Our private, personal prayers should be a time to share our deepest hurts and joys with Christ. They are not a time to complain, seek our own will, or put on a show for others. Jesus died to make a way for you to enter into God's presence, "And Jesus cried out again with a loud voice, and yielded up His spirit. Then, behold, the veil of the temple was torn in two from top to bottom; and the earth quaked, and the rocks were split" (Matt. 27:50-51). When we enter into God's holy sanctuary, our hearts and our thoughts should be responding to God's invitation to come before him in prayer, and then falling on our faces, seeking forgiveness, strength, and his will for our life. *What is man that God should bestow such an honor on him?*

Our Intercessory Prayer for Others

In Jesus' intercessory prayers, he was very specific about who and what he prayed for. We too are to be specific when we are interceding for others. Jesus prayed specifically that his Father would keep those he had given him, "That the saying might be fulfilled which He spoke, "Of those whom You gave Me I have lost none" (John 18:19). What a valuable lesson to learn. Do not hesitate to pray the Scriptures back to God, or to remind him of his promises. Not that he forgets, but God cannot deny himself. And by reminding him of his own spoken Word you establish your knowledge, understanding, and respect for him and his Word.

Jesus asked his Heavenly Father to fill the hearts of those who love him with joy, to protect them from the evil one, and to sanctify them. Being sanctified, by the Word of God, means you have the knowledge of the Son of God. You believe that Jesus was sent by God and you now desire God's will for your life. John MacArthur wrote in his commentary on John 17, "The idea of sanctification is the setting a part of something for a particular use. Accordingly, believers are set apart by God for His purposes alone so that the believer does only what God wants and hates all that God hates."

God has a simply wonderful plan and purpose for each one of his children, but in order to realize that purpose we must stay planted firmly in Christ. Without a right relationship with Jesus, we cannot do anything in the spiritual realm. Those who lose their way; thus, being separated from the true vine—Christ--wander from place to place, ministry to ministry, and from church to church never realizing their true potential in Christ.

What separates the branches from the vine? Sin and apathy toward the things of God! What is the result of such actions? We become drenched in denial. Trying to convince ourselves that what we are doing is not sin and nobody is going to find us out. The result of such actions causes separation from the Lord and the Body of Christ. Sin causes us to drown in a world of apathy and failures. We become depressed, negative, complaining, and criticizing. We alone have created this separation from God. So how do we get back in fellowship with him? We humbly go before God and seek his forgiveness. After sincerely repenting of our foolishness, how does God respond? He forgives our sins and cleanses us. I love the concept of cleansing. Once again you are squeaky clean in the eyes of the Lord. All, spots and stains, guilt and shame, have been removed and you have a new lease on life. To obtain this heavenly cleansing all you have to do is confess your wrongs and God faithfully forgives you and cleanses you,

> If we say that we have no sin, we deceive ourselves, and the truth is not in us. If we confess our sins, He is faithful and just to forgive us *our* sins and to cleanse us from all unrighteousness. If we say that we have not sinned we make Him a liar and His word is not in us (1 John 1:8-10, italics theirs).

In Jesus' intercessory prayers, he prayed for those who are still walking in darkness. We too should be interceding for those who do not know Christ. Just like the thief that came to Jesus while dying on the cross next to him found forgiveness. As long as there is life there is hope. Never give up praying for the lost souls of the world. In Jesus' intercessory prayer lies a mandate for Believers to verbally share the good news of Christ with others, "I do not pray for these alone, but also for those who will believe in Me through their word (John 17:20).

John MacArthur in his commentary on Jesus' intercessory prayer outlined three categories that he titled High Priestly Prayer (we are priests in the Kingdom of God). I think it goes a long way in answering the question; how do I prepare myself to do spiritual warfare for others:

Verses 1-5 Jesus first prays for Himself,

- He affirms the glory of the cross (vv. 1, 2): looking to the cross for the forgiveness of sins: Where new life begins.
- He expresses the very essence of eternal life (vv. 3, 4): this gift of eternal life originates at the cross.
- He rejoices in the shared glory of the Father (v.5). : identifying Himself as the second part of the Trinity.

In verses 6-19 Jesus prays for His disciples,

- He prays for their knowledge (vv. 6-9): the knowledge of the son of God, the one sent, to take away the sins of the world through faith in Jesus.
- He prays for their perseverance (vv. 10-12): for the continued work that Jesus started: sharing the good news (the Word) with others.
- He prays for their joy (v. 13): giving us the unspeakable joy that comes from a life redeemed.

- He prays for sanctification (vv. 14-17): that they would be set apart from the world protected and justified.
- He prays for their mission (vv. 18, 19): to complete the work that Jesus started.

In verses 20-26 Jesus prays for future believers,

- He prays for their oneness (vv. 20-22): being one with the Father, with Jesus and with one another, as the Body of Christ.
- He prays for their perfect unity (v. 23): in one accord.
- He prays for their future presence with Him (vv. 24, 25): Christ's desire is to spend eternity with His chosen ones.
- He prays for their mutual love (v. 26): the love of God will be in us that we will love each other as Christ has loved us. – John MacArthur

Visualize in your mind how to utilize these categories as a guide to make you more confident and effective in your intercessory prayers? I believe intercessory prayer is one of the greatest evangelistic tools at our disposal. When we are successful interceding for the salvation of others, we are changing the direction of their life and the direction of the church. There is no nobler Christian ministry than that.

If you wish to go deeper, read and meditate on the Lord's Prayer, Matthew 6:9, and read John 17. Then refer back to John MacArthur's outline on how to strengthen your intercessory prayers. Make your own outline on ways to improve your intercessory prayer life. List the names of those you want to intercede for and the targeted need or needs you want to pray for. Follow that outline and begin to do spiritual battle for those God has put on your heart. Keep track of answered prayer.

Chapter 14

Striving for Completeness
in Forgiveness

I believe hanging on to un-forgiveness is one of the devils quiet life destroyers. I am convinced that if we do not completely free ourselves of un-forgiveness we will not experience the abundance of joy from serving the Lord that we long for. Not only is it important to free ourselves of un-forgiveness, but we must offer that forgiveness in a biblical way so that the forgiveness we give will be a lasting forgiveness.

Has the forgiveness you extended to others truly been biblical forgiveness? Have you ever told someone, "I forgive you" and then brought what should have been forgiven up later to use against them? Have you granted forgiveness to someone and then in gruesome detail described the wrong you suffered to someone else? Or maybe after saying, "I forgive you" you found yourself thinking about that despicable act continuously causing anger and bitterness to rise up in your heart--all over again?

In this chapter, we are going to learn about the three types of forgiveness a Christian must grant in order to grow spiritually, and then we will examine the three-fold criteria which we can use to evaluate whether the forgiveness we have extended to others is truly biblical forgiveness.

I think we all agree that forgiveness is a beautiful idea until we have to practice it ourselves. Forgiveness is not something Christians can take lightly because forgiveness is clearly God's prescription for healing the brokenhearted. There is not one of us who has not been hurt deeply by someone we care about. No matter how great the offenses or abuses we endure somewhere along the path to healing lies forgiveness. Because at the very root of un-forgiveness lies pain. Pain that has been buried deep inside and the only way to get rid of that pain is to rip it out by the root. Un-forgiveness never lies dormant, but grows like a cancer in the heart. Which if untreated will destroy our lives and the lives of those we love. Harboring un-forgiveness, unknowingly, enables us to be our own worst enemy.

Christians must forgive because God commands us to because forgiveness is essential for our own healing. Forgiving others is a choice and forgiveness must come from the heart. We choose to forgive. Or we choose to hang on to the anger and bitterness of past hurts. The necessity to forgive is not limited to people. The human heart can *harbor* un-forgiveness towards employers, churches, government agencies, and other organizations. Hanging onto those types of un-forgiveness may be the most foolish of all. The Scriptures contain the prescription for lasting forgiveness, "Let all bitterness, wrath, anger, clamor, and evil speaking be put away from you, with all malice and be kind to one another, tenderhearted, forgiving one another, even as God in Christ forgave you" (Ephesians 4:31-32).

It is important to remember that we have hurt God and others and we too are in need of being forgiven. It is hypocrisy to expect God to forgive our sins and then refuse to forgive those who have sinned against us. If the desire of your heart is to be obedient to Christ's commands then forgiveness is not an option. You must forgive those who have harmed you.

Jesus, while hanging helplessly on the cross, and right before he took his last breath pleaded with his Father to forgive those who were killing him, "Father forgive them, for they know not what they do" (Luke 23:34). Those very same people, even after they heard Jesus' plea for God to forgive them continued to mock him and later cast lots for his clothing. Did those who stood by and cheered at his death deserve Jesus' forgiveness? Absolutely not, but Jesus chose to forgive them. And we must choose to forgive those who have hurt us in the past and be prepared to forgive those who will hurt us in the future. The act of forgiveness is a continuous process. A never ending practice, because people will continue to do things that will cause you pain.

The last thing Jesus did before he died was to grant forgiveness to a criminal dying on the cross next to him (cf. Luke 23:43). What a colossal moment that was: the beginning of forgiveness based on the sacrificial death of God's son. Have you forgiven someone who didn't deserve it? Someone who was unrepentant and refused to even admit the wrong they had done to you? Good for you. You are that much closer to being Christ-like!

I think there are some relevant clichés amongst Believers and one of them is, "Hurting people hurt people." That is so true. Another one is, "Pretending the hurt is not there or that it does not bother you will never bring healing." Facing your past and forgiving yourself and those who have hurt you is the only lasting solution. Forgiving breaks the cycle of anger! It does not settle all the questions of blame, justice, or fairness. God will do that someday. But it does allow you to heal and move forward in relationships.

Types Of Forgiveness

Forgiveness Extended From God to Us

The first and most important forgiveness is extended from God to us. I cannot pass up the opportunity to ask if you have accepted Christ's forgiveness for your sins. Or, maybe you have known the Lord in the past and have fallen away, but desire to reestablish that relationship. To get right with God, simply ask God for his forgiveness and he will happily grant it (cf. 1 John 1:9). To ask for God's forgiveness simple pray this prayer:

Dear Lord, I am a sinner, I am sorry for my sins; and I am asking you to forgive my sins and come into my heart and be the Lord of my life. From this day forward. In Christ's precious name I pray! Amen.

Accepting God's forgiveness is the first step in the process of forgiving others. It takes supernatural strength to give biblical forgiveness to those who have hurt you severely. The Scriptures teach that God places people right through their faith in Jesus Christ. We have all sinned and are in need of God's forgiveness (Romans 3:23). By the free gift of God's grace, sinners like you and me are justified through faith in Jesus Christ and invited to stand in God's holy presence. No matter how significantly we may have injured others or ourselves the grace of God is always sufficient to cover those sins. And the forgiveness we received must be accompanied by us forgiving those who have hurt us (cf. Matthew 6:14, 15).

Forgiveness Extended From Us to Others

Forgiving others is a process which takes time and commitment. Forgiving someone does not happen overnight; you must be willing, to be willing to forgive. In other words, you must make a choice to forgive; un-forgiveness never goes away on its own. You may have forgotten about a person or organization that has hurt you. But just because you do not think about it does not mean the damage it caused has gone away. The mind has a way of acting out certain destructive behaviors caused by forgotten hurts. For instance, if you run into a person, or come in contact with an organization that has caused you pain. At the moment of that encounter, suppressed anger rises up in you like volcanic ash out of a boiling volcano. The resurrected anger and bitterness makes it feel like the injustice just happened yesterday.

My home was broken into and ransacked and several things were stolen. I had a real good idea of who did it, but I had no proof. As the years went by, I did not think about the break-in all that much. But one day I ran into the person I was sure stole from me and the anger and downright hatred I felt for that person swelled up in me like I had just walked into my vandalized home moments before. I was a Christian now and the rekindling of those angry, hateful feelings made me feel small. I thought. "Lord, how can I be a Christian and feel that much hate toward someone?" I began to doubt the sincerity of my faith and Satan played havoc with me because of that. I began to pray for that person's salvation and finally I was able to truly forgive that person and put the pain of that experience behind me. I do not know if praying for that person changed them, but I do know it changed me.

Think about who your anger is hurting. I'll give you a hint. It's you! Refusing to grant forgiveness to others is like digesting cyanide and expecting the other person to slowly croak. Offering forgiveness enables you to free yourself of hurtful, angry feelings that have been lurking in the recesses of you mind and allows you to move forward positively in those relationships.

The Bible has a lot to say about forgiveness. In Romans 12:17, 18, Paul wrote, "Do not repay evil for evil. Be careful to do what is right in the eyes of everybody as far as it depends on you, live at peace with everyone." That Scripture teaches that we are not to repay evil for evil and that can be a struggle when you harbor feelings of anger and un-forgiveness. But we must resist the sinful desire to even the score. Feelings of anger, bitterness, revenge, and malice will destroy you. Are you harboring un-forgiveness towards a person, a group of persons, or an organization? If so, make that all-important Christ-like decision and grant to them your forgiveness.

Forgiving others in the eyes of God is simply not an option. In Matthew 6:14, 15 Jesus taught his disciples the importance of forgiving and the consequences of refusing to forgive, "For if you forgive men their trespasses, your heavenly Father will also forgive you. But if you do not forgive men their trespasses, neither will your heavenly Father forgive your trespasses." Jesus understood the necessity of forgiving those who injure us and left us with an example of his divine character when he forgave those who murdered him.

How can we justify un-forgiveness towards others and at the same time expect to receive God's forgiveness?

I know through my own personal experience that forgiving those who have hurt you is not easy. But God gives us no wiggle room. I said earlier that forgiving is a choice. So what is the true choice? Isn't it; I choose to forgive those who have harmed me because I choose to obey God's Word. The deepest and most complete healing begins with the choice to forgive.

The Bible says that God removes our sin as far as the east is from the west and promises to never use our repented sins against us or even bring those miscues up again. To truly forgive like God forgives commit to these three maxims:

- I will not use someone's past sins against them in the future, especially when disagreeing with them.
- I will not keep dwelling on the wrongs I have suffered.
- Nor will I speak of them to someone else.

The only way to begin to feel right toward another person is to begin to do right towards that person and to keep the threefold promise that you make when you say, "I forgive you."

Forgiving God

God does not and cannot sin; his very nature is marked by perfect holiness in every attribute and action. God is perfect in love, mercy, and grace. But remember he loves us so much that he gave us free will. He did not want a bunch of mindless puppets pretending to love him. He wants us to love him because he is our creator and he loves us. The ultimate free will God has given us is the free will to choose where we will spend eternity. God gives every soul the opportunity to make the right choice. You have free will to choose the glorious Light of Christ for eternity or eternal darkness. You know what the right choice is so do not put it off any longer—choose Christ

It is crucial for your healing to understand the harm others have done to you was from them having free will to choose their actions. Their sinful actions were not God's will. God cannot be tempted to do evil, nor will he tempt anyone to do evil. Evil is conceived in the heart of mankind and manifested in sinful actions. Sinful behavior, including doing evil deeds, is a human choice, not God's, "Let no one say when he is tempted, "I am tempted by God"; for God cannot be tempted by evil, nor does He Himself tempt anyone. But each one is tempted when he is drawn away by his own desires and enticed" (James 1:13, 14).

Better understanding free will enables you to realize that your anger toward God has been misplaced. All the evil found in this world is from the enemy of your soul, Satan, who has set out to destroy every life he can and he will use any means available to him to accomplish that goal, which includes using people. Jesus spoke of the choices you have: you can choose the true door that leads to life or you can choose the wrong door that leads to death, "I am the door. If anyone enters by Me, he will be saved, and will go in and out and find pasture. The thief does not come except to steal, and to kill, and to destroy. I have come that they may have life and that they may have *it* more abundantly" (John 10:9, 10, italics theirs).

I believe that most of us have heard the story of Jonah and how God commanded him to precede to Nineveh and preach repentance to the Ninevites. God made it clear to Jonah that if the people of Nineveh did not repent he was going to bring down fire and brimstone from heaven and destroy the whole city and every living soul in it. God wanted to give them a chance to be saved just like he gives us that chance. But Jonah refused to go. He chose to run from God; thinking he could hide from him—how foolish. Running from God is never a good idea. As we all know, Jonah ran but he could not hide. God deposited him in the belly of a big fish and after three days Jonah found himself back on dry ground; wondering, I imagine, what just happened. While in the belly of that fish, God gave Jonah a glimpse of what horrors await those who choose to be separated from God for all eternity (cf. Jonah 2:1-10).

Has God ever placed you in the belly of a big fish; after refusing to do what he wanted you to do? I have experienced the awfulness of such a place and it is not a lot of fun. To put that situation in a more modern term—it is like being between a rock and a hard place with no way to escape. Whenever you find yourself in a tough situation, especially when brought on by your own disobedience remember that God has made a way for you to escape--if you will just ask him to help you (cf.1 Corinthians 10:13).

Jonah hated the people of Nineveh and he knew because of God's mercy that God would forgive them if they repented. And that is exactly what happened. After three days in the belly of the fish--Jonah had a change of heart. I think most of us would! He decided it would be to his best interest to do what God instructed him to do. I think some of us have trouble coming to that conclusion sometimes. We believe we can hide from God and do things our own way. We always find out in the long run that we were wrong. Doing it God's way is always best. Doing things our own way always makes matters worse.

In the Book of Jonah, chapter 4, verse 1, it says, "Because God forgave the Ninevites Jonah became angry with God." In verse 4 God asks Jonah, "Is it right for you to be angry at me?" I was angry at God for many years. The more miserable my life became the angrier towards him I became. I wanted to blame God for every bad choice I made and every bad choice that those who hurt me made. Once I began to understand the love God had for me, and that I am, and you are, the reason God sent his son Jesus Christ to die a horrible death on the cross; is when I realized God loved me in spite of how rotten I was! That insight into God's heart changed my life. If you are feeling anger towards God it will be to your benefit to sit down and ask yourself the very question God asked Jonah "Is it right for you to be angry at God?" The answer will always be it is never right to harbor anger or un-forgiveness toward God. God is a holy, righteous being and only wants what is best for you. Allow him to speak into your life and you will see the deepest and truest love you will ever know or experience.

Although we do not always understand the hardships we have to endure. We need to understand that God's promises are sure and that he loves us. In 1Peter 5:10, God promises that he is with you through your trials and he will use them to make you more like his son Jesus, "The God of all grace, who called us to His eternal glory by Christ Jesus after you have suffered awhile, will perfect, establish, strengthen, and settle you." One giant step in the process of completeness--spiritual maturity--is found in forgiving God and others.

Forgiving Ourselves

The last kind of forgiveness is perhaps the most difficult for us to extend. We need to forgive ourselves. Have you forgiven yourself over past mistakes? You can forgive God and others. You can accept God's forgiveness, but you may feel the guilt and shame of your past is just too much for you to forgive. When we say we cannot forgive ourselves, we are really saying I cannot put behind me the shame and guilt of the past. I struggled with that very thing early in my Christian walk. How could I forgive myself for the devastation I caused? Until a very wise man reminded me that God never commands us to forgive ourselves. The Bible says that we are to ask forgiveness from others (cf. Matthew 5:23-24). We are to ask God to forgive us (cf. 1 John 1:9). We are to forgive others (cf. Matthew 6:14-15). The Bible teaches that we are to love God, others, ourselves, and even our enemies. But the Bible never tells us to forgive ourselves. Why is that? Because when Christ cried out from the cross, "It is finished," it was finished. Jesus took our sin, our shame, and our guilt and all we have to do to receive that cleansing is to accept that forgiveness by faith. What a simple solution to mankind's depravity.

If we persist in living in the past, by refusing to accept Christ's work on the cross for the forgiveness our own sins. And insist on holding on to un-forgiveness towards ourselves; we are basically saying that Christ's sacrifice was not good enough to cover those sins. That there needs to be something more done. I assure you that the precious Blood of Christ is sufficient for the forgiveness of sins. God did not send his son to die a horrible death so we can carry the shame and guilt of the past around. No, Jesus gave his life so that we can be free of that very guilt and shame. Are you carrying shame and guilt around with you? It's quite heavy, isn't it? If you are still carrying around the weight of shame and guilt, cast those burdens upon the Lord's shoulders and let him cleanse your soul (cf. Matthew 11:28-30).

I do not have anything against the concept of needing to forgive ourselves, but it is important for those who cannot move on to understand that Christ paid the price for your sins. Let me ask you a question. If God can forgive you, how can you withhold forgiveness from yourself? Are your standards higher than his? It is foolishness to carry around the shame and guilt of your past. If you hang onto the sins of the past the enemy of your soul will beat you to death with it. Christ's sacrificial death on the cross frees us from living life in a state of regret. The Apostle Paul wrote in Philippians 3:13, 14, "One thing I do, forgetting those things which are behind and reaching forward to those things which are ahead. I press toward the goal for the prize of the upward call of God in Christ Jesus."

Make the freedom choice and put-off the shame and guilt of your past life. Remember, once you gave your life to Christ you became a brand new shiny person cleansed from all past sins (cf. 2 Corinthians 5:17). You will never experience the complete blessings of God if you hang onto the past. It is for sure you can do nothing to change the mistakes you have made. Christians. We cannot allow ourselves to bury the joy of the Lord in the aftermath of past mistakes. Instead we must allow the joy of the Lord to shine through us as we prepare to serve Christ in the future.

Nothing we do can cleanse us from sin; only God can do that through the precious Blood of Christ. What we can do is accept his cleansing. The prophet Isaiah put it this way, "Come let's talk this over! Says the Lord; no matter how deep the stain of your sins, I can take it out and make you clean as freshly fallen snow. Even if you are stained as red as crimson, I can make you white as wool; *If you will only let me help you*" (Isaiah 1:18, 19, italics mine).

Let us, let God, help us today. Jesus' death on the cross was the ultimate act of forgiveness. As I mentioned from the beginning, holding un-forgiveness toward God, others, or yourself can seriously hinder your walk with Christ. Choose to make the right choice and accept God's forgiveness. Forgive God those who have hurt you, and forgive yourself.

If you desire to go deeper read Matthew chapters 5, 6, 7, paying close attention to the verses on forgiveness. Make a confidential list-- for your eyes only--of those you need to forgive and start praying for them. If you are burdened by the wrongs you have done to others, if possible, and will not cause harm to you or others ask for their forgiveness.

Chapter 15

Striving for Completeness in Thankfulness

Many falsely assume that being a Christian exempts them from struggles; but the truth is no one escapes trials and tribulations. The difference between a Christian and a non-Christian, in life's struggles, is that Jesus walks alongside a Christian through those trials giving them strength, while a non-believer dredges through them on their own strength. God will never abandon his children for any reason, except sin, "*Let your* conduct *be* without covetousness; *be* content with such things as you have. For He Himself has said, *"I will never leave you nor forsake you"* (Hebrews 13:5, italics theirs).

God's desire is to experience life with you, and to lavish on you all the blessings that come from a life shared with him. In the Old Testament, God was ready to hand over to his chosen people a land flowing with milk and honey (cf. Exodus 3:8). But God was not going to give them this beautiful land unless they showed him they were worthy of such a generous gift--they had to prove they were trustworthy. All they needed to do to receive this gorgeous land was to obey his commandments. God tested them. But they failed the test because of fear, they were afraid to move forward to possess the land because of the opposition they faced, which caused them to question God's ability to protect them and fulfil his promises to them. Does God still test us today? Yes. God tested the children of Israel to see where their hearts were and he will test you to see where your heart is.

How different might history have been if the nation of Israel had trusted God and showed their gratefulness instead of constantly complaining? Have you gone through tough times that were made worse because of a lack of gratitude towards God? How often should Christians give thanks to God? 1Thessalonians 5:18 says, "In everything give thanks for this is the will of God in Christ Jesus." Scripture instructs us to give thanks in everything no matter what the situation, especially in hard times. I truly believe that joy flows out of a thankful heart. When your heart is filled with gratitude and hope, you cannot help but feel joy. The Bible teaches that the joy of the Lord is our strength. What are you grateful for today? Make a list, present it to God, and let him know how thankful a person you are for what he has done for you.

I have put together a nonexclusive list of things the Scriptures teach us to express our thankfulness for:

- Food (provisions): Whether it is manna or a T-bone steak; we are to give thanks for our food, "Jesus broke the loaves and when He had given thanks He distributed them to the disciples" (John 6:11).
- Converts: We are to thank God for other Believers, "We give thanks to God always for you all, making mention of you in our prayers" (1 Thessalonians. 1:2).
- Answered prayer: We are to thank God for answered prayer, "Jesus lifted up His eyes and said, "Father, I thank You that You have heard Me" (John 11:41).
- Victory: We are to thank God for victory over sin, "The sting of death is sin, and the strength of sin is the law. But thanks be to God who gives us the victory through our Lord Jesus Christ" (1 Cor. 15:56-57).

- Salvation: We are to give God thanks for our salvation, "Thanks be to God for His indescribable gift!" (2 Cor. 9:15).
- Changed lives: We are to thank God for changed lives: for the work he has done in our life and in the lives of others, "For this reason we also thank God without ceasing, because when you received the word of God which you heard from us, you welcomed *it* not *as* the word of men, but as it is in truth, the word of God, which also effectively works in you who believe" (1 Thess. 2:13, italics theirs).

We are to give thanks during our trials because it is the testing of our faith that matures us into a person that Jesus can use to minister to others. I believe that God gives us moments of unspeakable joy to record in our memories so we can draw on them when times are difficult. As we draw on those precious memories, and recall how God worked during those difficult times to strengthen us. It allows us to minister to others as they go through trials. After difficult trials, I have discovered that God allows a time for us to rest and reflect on his goodness and faithfulness. This God given time of reflection and refreshing rejuvenates our souls and heals our wounds before he sends us back onto the spiritual battlefield.

As important as it is to be thankful during the good times, it is even more important to give thanks during the tough times. Are you still giving thanks when things are not going your way? Or do you begin to grumble, doubting God's promises? The redeemed of God should be the most grateful of any people, even in suffering, because of the personal relationship they have with Christ. I think it goes without saying that all of us have areas in our lives where we can be more thankful. If you had a score card of how grateful a person you are from 1-10 where would score? In areas where you scored low, would you be willing to make Christ-honoring changes? List the areas in your life where you need to be more thankful and commit to making positive changes in those areas.

Is God happy with persons who are unthankful? Numbers

11:1 gives a pretty good description of how the Lord feels about individuals or nations who are ungrateful, "Now when the people complained, it displeased the Lord; for the Lord heard it, and His anger was aroused." Nothing destroys a person's joy as fast as being ungrateful. Have you lost some of your joy? Could it be because of an unthankful heart?

When we become ungrateful, we begin to moan, groan, and complain; and we all know where that attitude comes from. Is complaining one of God's attributes? No. An ungrateful attitude comes from the enemy of your soul. The devil does not want you to show your thankfulness towards God when times are hard, because thankfulness flings open the gates to the very throne of God for us to enter—a place where Satan dare not tread.

What is the prerequisite for being in the presence of the Lord? Answer. Being thankful! "Enter into His gates with thanksgiving, *And* into His courts with praise. Be thankful to Him, *and* bless His name" (Psalm 100:4, italics theirs). What is the biblical cure for the stress and anxiety in today's culture? It comes down to how thankful we are. The Apostle Paul wrote in Philippians 4:6, "Be anxious for nothing, but in everything by prayer and supplication, *with thanksgiving*, let your requests be made known to God" (Italics mine).

Melody Beattie said this about gratitude,

> "Gratitude unlocks the fullness of life. It turns what we have into enough, and more. It turns denial into acceptance, chaos to order, confusion to clarity. It can turn a meal into a feast, a house into a home, a stranger into a friend. Gratitude makes sense of our past, brings peace for today, and creates a vision for tomorrow."

There is so much truth in that quote which speaks directly to the success of our Christian walk. Gratitude unlocks the fullness of life: we were lost in our sins before we accepted Christ as our Lord and Savior, and apart from that relationship we cannot live a full life. Gratitude transforms our denial into acceptance: we are accepted into God's family becoming joint heirs with Christ and receiving all the blessings that are ours through our communion with Christ. Gratitude brings chaos to order and confusion to clarity. How much does chaos and confusion control your life? I was drowning in chaos and confusion until I allowed Jesus to take control of my choices. Gratitude helps us make sense of our past: knowing Christ places the broken pieces of our past into their proper places and gives us confidence to move forward. Finally, gratitude creates a vision for tomorrow: "Where there is no vision the people parish" (Proverbs 28:18).

Showing gratitude and giving forgiveness go hand-in-hand. Unless the two are done simultaneously the result will be a heart confused and filled with uncertainty. Those who have an unthankful heart always seem to search out what is wrong and are quick to judge others and find fault. Except when it comes to them; instead, they turn a blind-eye to their own faults and blame everyone else for their problems. This one simple biblical principle--always giving thanks—if followed would work miracles in the lives of people, and quickly change society for the better.

A thankful heart does not happen overnight. Wouldn't it be great if after we become a Christian we would automatically overflow with thankfulness? That may have happened for you, but for me, after becoming a Christ follower, I still had a lot of Christian maturing to do before I truly understood the importance of giving thanks in everything.

Let's finish this chapter with a Psalm of Thanksgiving:

> Make a joyful shout to the LORD, all you lands!
> Serve the LORD with gladness;
> Come before His presence with singing.
> Know that the LORD, He *is* God;

It is He *who* has made us, and not we ourselves;
We are His people and the sheep of His pasture.
Enter into His gates with thanksgiving,
And into His courts with praise.
Be thankful to Him, *and* bless His name.
For the LORD *is* good;
His mercy *is* everlasting,
And His truth *endures* to all generations" (Psalm 100,
italics theirs)

If you desire to go deeper, memorize Psalm 100 and place it on the mirror, or wherever you can see it on a daily basis and put what it says into practice every day.

Chapter 16

Striving for Completeness
in Knowing God

How do you visualize God in your mind? Pause for a moment and think about that question. When attempting to understand who God is, it is important to understand that God is a spirit and not made-up of flesh. Jesus said in John 4:24, "God *is* Spirit, and those who worship Him must worship in spirit and truth" (Italics theirs). The purest form of worship happens when we disengage from the flesh and worship God in the spirit of holiness. No flesh will enter into the presence of God. We come to him, and speak to him, through the authority of the Holy Spirit. As we worship in his presence, we feel freedom from life's trouble and gain confidence knowing in our heart that we have access to the very throne of God.

God is everywhere at all times. Heaven cannot contain him, nor can the lower parts of the earth keep him out. The vastness of the ocean is like a mud puddle to God. He soars through the heavens at will. Therefore, we must not place boundaries on him or limit his power to do the impossible, "For with God nothing will be impossible" (Luke 1:37).

Visualizing God as that great grandfather figure in the sky, which many in today's society do, is an awful misconception of who God is. God is not there to grant you your every wish. Nor will he make excuses for your sins. But rather he has made a way for your sins to be covered by the precious Blood of Jesus Christ. Why doesn't God always give us what we ask for? After all, the Bible says that God will give you the desires of your heart, "Delight yourself also in the LORD, And He shall give you the desires of your heart (Psalm 37:4). Did you catch the stipulation? "Delight yourself also in the LORD." When we give God our deepest devotion, in his timing, he will give us the desires of our heart according to his will--not ours.

Most of the time our desires are not what is best for us. What do you call a child that gets everything they want? You might describe such a child as a spoiled brat. God is more interested in what we need in order to grow into the likeness of his son Jesus than what we want. Remember, every luxury, every good gift, is waiting for you when you enter the gates of heaven, "The twelve gates *were* twelve pearls: each individual gate was of one pearl. And the street of the city *was* pure gold, like transparent glass" (Revelation 21:21, italics theirs). All the riches of heaven are waiting for the heirs of Jesus Christ--whom you are.

Some, mistakenly, view God as this mean, demanding task master standing over them with a whip in his hand punishing them and keeping them from having any fun; constantly telling them what they can and cannot do. That is a lie straight from the devils mouth. God only wants what is best for his children, "Every good gift and every perfect gift is from above, and comes down from the Father of lights, with whom there is no variation or shadow of turning" (James 1:17). God does not force his children to submit to him through physical punishment, but reaches them through the love of Jesus. Who suffered God's punishment, for sin, so we do not have to.

The commandments God has given to humankind are there to protect them from doing harm to themselves through their own sinful desires. Sin always injures. Sin never harms just the sinner it harms everyone around them, especially the ones who love them.

The human race, even though they refuse to admit it, is on a fast track toward self-destruction because of their rebellion against God and his commandments. That rebellion is being fueled by the secular misconception of who God is. If God is doing anything in heaven he is shedding tears for the lost souls who refuse to accept his grace and mercy. God weeps over the suffering and harm human beings have caused to the earth and to each other because of their refusal to gain biblical knowledge of him and his ways. As Jesus rode into Jerusalem, on Palm Sunday, he cried, and he still sheds those same tears today as he looks down and sees the depravity happening in the world today. God help us!

God is not made of flesh but he came to earth in the form of flesh in the incarnation of the Lord Jesus Christ, "And the Word became flesh and dwelt among us, and we beheld His glory, the glory as of the only begotten of the Father, full of grace and truth" (John 1:14). It was a vital part of God's plan of redemption for him to understand firsthand the struggles of humanity apart from his divine character: to live among us and feel the same physical pain, emotional pain, and experience the same temptations humans' experience. How else could God judge the human race without prejudice? Jesus experienced every temptation we have been tempted with but Jesus never sinned, "For we do not have a High Priest who cannot sympathize with our weaknesses, but was in all points tempted as we are, yet without sin" (Hebrews 4:15).

Jesus is the Holy and Righteous Judge and God has placed all judgment into his hands. Jesus knows the joys of life, the sufferings of life, and every ugly aspect of the human heart. And that is why he can judge righteously, "For the Father judges no one, but has committed all judgement to the Son" (John 5:22). Placing the judgment of the human race into Jesus' hand demonstrates how important justice is to God. I feel sorry for those who do not know the loving touch of God, the purity of his character, or his love for justice and mercy.

Through the incarnation of Christ--God in the flesh--Jesus was able, once and for all, to crucify the flesh with all its corruption. Christ's death on the cross allows each human being the opportunity, in the name of Jesus, to be reborn a new creation. Jesus experienced all the physical pain of humanness: hunger, thirst, the harshness of heat and cold, and of torture and death. Jesus experienced the emotional pain of being separated from his earthly family; his brothers thought he was crazy. He felt the sting of betrayal and abandonment from his friends; Judas betrayed him and his disciples all fled at his arrest. In all four gospels, Peter refused to admit he even knew Jesus (cf. Matthew 26, Mark, 14, Luke 22, John 18). Jesus felt the agonizing torment of spiritual pain, as his beloved Heavenly Father turned his back at the very moment the sins of the whole world were being dumped on his shoulders. God cannot look upon sin and for that historical moment God looked away from his precious Son. I was not there, but I am sure there were tears streaming down God's face as his son hung there in such pain. Those tears of sorrow were soon followed by tears of joy at the completion of his plan to redeem mankind. Jesus despised the shame of the cross, but endured the horrors of the cross for the joy that would bring the salvation of so many (cf. Hebrews 12:2).

Jesus, in the Gospel of John, while talking to Nicodemus, describes the Holy Spirit as the wind which comes and goes but is not seen. The Holy Spirit moves throughout the earth, without difficulty, completing the work Jesus has instructed him to finish. The Spirit of God is like the wind, which you cannot see, but you can feel the Spirit's gentle breeze or His correcting whirlwind-- depending on which one is needed. As you walk in unison with the Holy Spirit, you have no doubt of his existence,

> That which is born of the flesh is flesh, and that which is born of the Spirit is spirit. "Do not marvel that I said to you, 'You must be born again.' "The wind blows where it wishes, and you hear the sound

of it, but cannot tell where it comes from and where
it goes. So is everyone who is born of the Spirit
(John 3:6--8).

We understand that a spirit is without physical limitations. By our
own experience, we also know that the physical body has limitations.
Although God created the human body a perfect specimen, sin got
in the way. And because of sin the body was cursed along with all
creation and condemned to deteriorate and die. Our physical death
did not happen because God wanted to destroy our bodies, but was
a result of our own sinfulness.

God formed the human body from the dust of the earth. Now
worthless for heavenly use, so what makes our bodies so precious to
God that he would send Jesus to die to save us? It is not the body
that is valuable, but the soul which lives inside the body. The soul
belongs to God and lives forever, "Behold, all souls are mine; the
soul of the father as well as the soul of the son is mine; the soul who
sins shall die" (Ezekiel 18:4).

In order for us to be perfect, the flesh must be destroyed and the
soul must be redeemed. After death we will be given a new spiritual
body for the soul to take up residence in; a perfect and complete
body without sin, and indeed unable to sin, then we will truly be
like Christ—perfect, "Beloved, now we are children of God; and it
has not yet been revealed what we shall be, but we know that when
He is revealed, we shall be like Him, for we shall see Him as He is"
(1 John 3:2).

Your soul is going to live on into eternity. If folks really understood
the significance of an eternity separated from God churches would
be busting at the seams with people seeking salvation. The soul will
move on to eternity, while the body stays here to be mixed in with
the dust of the earth. I must ask the question. Where will your soul
be after your body dies? Will it be in heaven enjoying God for all
eternity, or end up in the lower parts of the earth being tormented
forever?

When we hear the word spirit, we have a tendency to reduce it to our level of understanding: putting it neatly away in a place where we will not have to deal with its eternal destination. Ignoring the fact that someday the body is going to cease to function and the part that lives on has only two places to go; will not diminish our responsibility to reject or accept God's offer of salvation. We have already established that God is just; he cannot lie, nor ignore sin. He will not change his mind on the Day of Judgment. If your name is not written in the Book of Life, those who have received Christ, through faith, your soul will be condemned to a dark, dark place separated from God for all eternity. Please do not let that happen without giving God a chance to prove to you that he lives; that he loves you, and wants to spend eternity with you. Jesus' promise, "Behold, I stand at the door and knock. If anyone hears My voice and opens the door, I will come in to him and dine with him, and he with Me" (Revelation 3:20).

Billy Graham said this about the Spirit, as described in the Scriptures,

> We do know that the spirit is not something that is bound in a body. Spirit is not wearable as a body. Spirit is not changeable as a body. The Bible declares that God is such a Spirit—that he is not limited to body; He is not limited to shape; He is not limited to boundaries or bonds; He is absolutely immeasurable and undiscernible by eyes that can see only physical.

God has no limitations, he is everywhere all at the same time, he hears and sees everything, and he knows everything. David describes God's omnipresence in Psalm 139:7, "Where can I go from Your Spirit? Or where can I flee from Your presence?" The Holy Spirit with all its power and magnificence lives inside of each Believer, "But if the Spirit of Him who raised Jesus from the dead dwells in you, He who raised Christ from the dead will also give life to your mortal bodies through His Spirit who dwells in you" (Romans 8:11).

If the Christian community is ever able to completely grasp and embrace that biblical truth it could truly be said, "God's greatest revival has arrived." But the reality is, in our humanness, we are not able to completely comprehend the power available to us through the Holy Spirit. Or we try to manufacture that power through human abilities. Jesus understood that power and how to use it. That is why he was able to do so many miracles: he understood God completely and how to use God's Spirit to accomplish the work his Father sent him to do. We let our doubt and sinfulness get in the way of unleashing the full potential of the Holy Spirit within us.

The Scriptures inform us that God loves, that he speaks, that he hears, that he weeps, that he laughs, he gets angry, and he hates evil. Not people. God possesses the attributes we attribute to a person. A human feels, thinks, cries, laughs, has desires, shows a distinct personality, and so does God. God is not bound by a body but he has the traits that are part of a person; but without the flaws that plague the human character. God is a perfect *being*, as demonstrated by Jesus' life: God's love is perfect, God's *will* and desires are perfect, God's feelings, thoughts, and actions are perfect. The Bible describes God as a consuming fire, which by instinct, we would all flee from. The magnificence and power of God is so hard to comprehend, but when we visualize God in the context of human attributes it helps us put him in perspective: in a place where we can feel more comfortable speaking with him. It is easier to approach God on a human level. When we perceive God as a person, with the same characteristics as us, it helps us relate to him.

God is a Holy and Righteous being; visualize his face sparkling like a radiant star that shines so brightly in the heavens. I wonder if it was his face looking down from heaven, to gaze upon his son, the shepherds saw twinkling in the night sky that first Christmas. The Bible teaches that God's light is so bright that in the world to come we will have no need for the sun or moon for God's light shall shine so brightly it will be all the light we will ever need, "The city had no need of the sun or of the moon to shine in it, for the glory of God illuminated it, The Lamb *is* its light" (Rev. 21:23, italics theirs).

The very throne of God is established on the basis of God's holiness. It was God's holiness which Jesus Christ was sent to earth to fulfill: to transfer the righteousness of Christ, through faith in him, to sinful humanity. Because of God's holiness, he cannot look upon sin and without the covering of Jesus there is no way for us to be in the presence of a holy God. Thus, on Christ's death, the veil was torn, throwing open the doors of the temple, allowing sinful man to enter into God's presence that for so many years was denied. Everything God has done has been for one purpose: to restore mankind into fellowship with himself.

Finally, God is love. Many people, including Christians, fail to recognize what is meant when the Scripture says that God is love, "And we have known and believed the love that God has for us. God is love, and he who abides in love abides in God, and God in him" (John 4:16). Jesus said, "The second greatest commandment of all is to love your neighbor as yourself" (cf. Mark 12:31). That is a tall order for people. When human beings look at other human beings, they judge them by their outward appearance. They judge from the outside in, which can create envy and jealousy. Those emotions can cause people to lust for what someone else has. When God looks at you, he looks at the heart. His holiness will not allow him to falsely judge or desire the things of this earth; thus, making his love perfect. God has no earthly agenda except to save mankind from self-destruction.

God looks at the inner man and realizes what he can become through Christ. The complete fulfillment of God's perfect love was witnessed on the cross. Only a perfect, unselfish, and sacrificial love would be willing to sacrifice the one person they love the most to save someone else. God openly displayed his perfect love, as he watched his only begotten son die for sinful humanity. God's perfect love for you and me provided the way of redemption for a sinful bunch of undeserving sinners, "God demonstrates His own love toward us, in that while we were still sinners, Christ died for us" (Romans 5:8).

Never question God's perfect love for you. It is as unchangeable as his holiness. No matter how dark your sin--God still loves you. God's love is everlasting and his love was established before the foundations of the world were laid. Find strength in these biblical truths no matter what happens: God has always loved you and God will never stop loving you.

Do you feel it is impossible to know God intimately? In reality, God is the easiest person to get to know. He has told us everything we need to know about him in the Scriptures. Once you hand over your life to God he takes up residence inside your heart and becomes part of you and you become part of him. The two become one! God's plan from the very beginning of creation was to fellowship with the people he created (cf. Genesis 3:8). God desires someone to love and for someone to love him back; God is not so complicated. Read his word and discover his perfect love for yourself.

Love is extremely powerful and God has so much love to give he created humans so he could shower them with that love. All the human race had to do was accept God's love; but instead, we rejected it. And look at the mess we are in today. In my lifetime, I have never seen an unhappier or more confused world. When I look at the condition of our great country, I truly hurt inside, as I think about the brave souls who sacrificed their lives for this country. I often wonder what they would say about the condition of America's heart today. In our nation's capital, no longer does justice and righteousness march in the halls; instead, abides all kinds of evil: hatred, greed, pride, gossipers, and people who are willing to destroy a life to get what they want.

We need God's presence in our country more now than ever before, "If My people who are called by My name will humble themselves, and pray and seek My face, and turn from their wicked ways, then I will hear from heaven, and will forgive their sin and heal their land" (2 Chronicles 7:14). It is in the power of the American people to turn this downward spiral around, through sincere repentance, prayer, and seeking God's help.

God does not care about political agendas. He cares about the heart condition of a nation and its people. He cares about righteousness, justice, loving others, loving God, taking care of the poor, and doing the things that are right in his sight. The priorities of this nation have been completely flipped around when compared to the Founding Father's outline for building a great nation--among all nations.

Why do I love God? Because he is worthy of my undivided love, and has proven to me over and over again how much he loves me. When God created us, he created us as perfect beings. And because of his love for us God gave each person free will to choose whether to love him back, or not. As usual, humans chose to love themselves more than God. Remember that God could have done away with us anytime he wanted to, but he chose to love us in spite of our rebellion. God offers to each individual an opportunity to turn their lives around through faith in his sinless son Jesus. Close examination of God's word leaves us with only two choices. First choice, yes, I accept a second chance and I want to spend eternity with God. The second choice, no, I refuse God's plan for salvation and I choose to spend eternity separated from God.

The God I know and love is kind and compassionate, always giving, never taking. His decisions for my life are always the correct decisions because they are not made out of selfish ambition, but are made out of a perfect love for me. I love God because he is the greatest friend anyone could have. He listens to me without interruption and he never judges me; although, he will judge the world someday. When I do wrong, God always gives me a chance to repent and do the right thing. He is patience and kind with me and is eager to forgive my shortcomings--when I sincerely ask for his forgiveness. The reason I ache inside with love for God is because he walks with me and talks with me every day. He has come down from heaven to fellowship with fallen human beings. All those years

I did everything I could to hurt him. Yet he still loved me and freely gave his life so that I might truly live. How can I not love a God like that with all of my heart?

I feel God's love and comfort wherever I go and whatever I do. You can have that same intimate relationship with God which deep down is what every human being desires--whether they will admit it or not. God has flung opened the doors of heaven for you to walk through by simply accepting his plan of salvation. Tell God this very moment you want that personal relationship with him and then begin to learn everything you can about him. The best place to start is by reading the Bible. Then continue growing spiritually, by developing a strong prayer life. And start attending a Bible believing church, and get involved in Christian ministry.

Begin to journal; I started journaling years ago. Writing down experiences on a daily basis helps in your spiritual growth and opens up a whole new line of communication between you and God. As you keep a daily record, you can better see the role God plays in your daily life; which gives you an accurate record of how intimately God has worked in your life. A journal allows you to look back and see how you have grown in your Christian walk and the areas you still need to work on. Personal letters are a *warm* way to communicate, and journaling is simply writing daily letters to the lord. Sharing personal thoughts with God allows you to grow closer and closer to him and will reveal a deeper understanding of him as he answers your letters by opening up the Scriptures (his return letter) to you on a more personal basis.

In order to grow to completeness—spiritual maturity—it is necessary to get involved. Join a Bible study group and attend regularly. Take training courses in Christian ministry that your church offers and volunteer to serve in those ministries. If you have the time, and can afford to take some college courses in Theology or Christin ministry—do so; getting a Christian education helped me grow spiritually. There are so many Christian education opportunities out there at very little cost if you will seek them out. Begin to read Christian authors, but make sure they are truly Christian authors and their writings are based on the Bible. The biggest mistake of all is to do nothing. Like anything worthwhile, growing into completeness in Christ takes action. The Lord said, "If you seek me you shall find me when you seek me with all your heart. Put all your heart, mind, and body into seeking God and you will not be disappointed.

I want to end this chapter with these verses about the depth of God's love,

> "Yet in all these things we are more than conquerors through Him who loved us. For I am persuaded that neither death nor life, nor angels nor principalities nor powers, nor things present nor things to come, nor height nor depth, nor any other created thing, shall be able to separate us from the love of God which is in Christ Jesus our Lord" (Romans 8:37-39).

If you desire to go deeper, take a few moments each day and meditate on the significance of those verses and ask God to fill your heart and life with his love. God is not going to force himself on you; although, in several different ways he does reveal himself to each person, but it is the responsibility of each individual to seek him out and learn of him, "You will seek me and find me, when you search for me with all your heart" (Jeremiah 29:13). Make a commitment to seek God with all of your heart.

Conclusion

While doing an interview with a newspaper reporter, I was asked, "How did you go from a drunk to a pastor?" I was dumbfounded when she asks me that question; because, I did not have an answer for her. I said, "I just got involved." I believe that is the key to a successful Christian life: to get involved in the church, be active in your Christian disciplines, read the Bible and pray daily, and take an active role in reaching the lost for Christ.

Over the years, I have felt like such a failure, and honestly, at times, I still do. I was a failure as a son, a father, a husband, and a friend. I began to think about what constitutes success or failure in life. Recently I was watching a Paul Newman movie and one of his lines was, "No one gets out of life alive." That hit home with me since I had been trying to answer some questions about success and failure. When it comes right down to it, in the end, we are all failures in this life. We all lose; we all die, and whatever success we have accomplished or whatever failure we turn out to be dies with us (cf. Ecclesiastes 1:1--4).

Success or failure in life cannot be judged by what you have accomplished or how many toys you have at the end of your life. But life must be measured by how you have lived your life and how you have ended your life. Have you given control of your life to Jesus and lived in a way that pleases him? The true measure of success in life is when you have breathed your last breath are you standing before the throne of God or are you somewhere else that is not very pleasant?

Contemplating on what constitutes success in life brought to mind the story Jesus told about Lazarus and the rich man in Luke 16:19--31. The rich man was adorned in fancy clothes and ate the finest foods and was esteemed by all. But Lazarus was a beggar, who had sores all over his body and was trying to just survive by eating the crumbs that fell from the rich man's table. Poor Lazarus even had to fight the dogs for the food that fell to the floor. Both Lazarus and the rich man die. Lazarus is taken to Abraham's bosom (a place of comfort while waiting on the return of Christ). While the rich man went to Hades (a place of great heat and torment). As the rich man looked up, he saw Lazarus being held by Abraham. The rich man, in his agony, cried out, "Father Abraham, have mercy on me, and send Lazarus that he may dip the tip of his finger in water and cool my tongue; for I am tormented in this flame" (Luke 16:24).

Abraham tells the rich man, "It is too late." You made your choice while on earth and there is nothing that can change the choice you made after you die. You are stuck in that horrible place of great torment for all eternity. And folks that is a long, long time. Then the rich man pleads for Lazarus to go tell his brothers to change their ways so that they do not end up in the clutches of such an awful place. Someone did return from the dead to warn us about the consequences of refusing God's invitation to escape eternal punishment. That person was the Lord Jesus Christ, who on the first Easter morning stepped out of the grave.

Mary Magdalene and the other women went to anoint Jesus' body after the Sabbath, as they approach Jesus' grave an angel of the Lord descended from heaven and rolled away the huge stone from the grave. The angel spoke to the women as they sought the Lord, "Do not be afraid I know that you seek Jesus who was crucified." Well, he's not here; for he has risen, as he said. Come see the place where the Lord lay" (Matthew 28:5, 6). How confused their hearts and minds must have been; but Jesus did not allow them remain confused. While the women were leaving, to go tell Jesus' disciple's about their encounter, Jesus revealed himself to them. Speaking encouragement to the women Jesus said, "Do not be afraid. Go and tell My brethren to go to Galilee, and there they will see me" (Matthew 28:10).

Are you going to listen to someone who came back from the dead, or are you going to ignore such a powerful witness by refusing to accept God's plan of salvation? The Bible teaches that it is assigned for a person to die once and then the judgement. God is a *just* God and cannot go back on his word. If you do not accept Christ as Lord and Savior, before you die, you will be in the same sinking boat as the rich man--it will be too late.

After reflecting on the story of Lazarus and the rich man, it became obvious to me who had the most success in their earthly life. Lazarus, with all of his poverty and sickness ended up having a successful life on earth because he was spending eternity in heaven with Jesus. On the other hand, the rich man who experienced all the luxuries this life provides ended up a failure in the end because his final destination was in a place of torment.

I hope as you have read this book that you do not think this book is about me, because that was not my intention. My purpose for this book was to give a personal testimony about a kind, faithful, forgiving, and loving God called Jesus Christ. And to thank him for rescuing me from a life of drunkenness and despair, and allowing me to experience a life of hope filled with love, joy, and peace. Thank you Lord Jesus! There is no greater proof of success in life then to serve the Lord Jesus Christ, and to be redeemed into the life to come.

There have been times of great despair, pain, and uncertainty in my life. But through it all I have enjoyed the life God has given me. I grew up in a time of great music; when rock 'n' roll, rocked the world: Elvis, the Beatles, the Rolling Stones, the Eagles, Credence Clearwater Revival, Woodstock and the birth of Motown: the Supremes, Marvin Gaye and Stevie Wonder--just to name a few. What glorious music came from those times? I lived in a time when true muscle cars ruled the highways: 427, Ford Mustangs, 396,

Chevy Chevelles, 327, Chevy, Camaro Z28's, 440, Dodge Chargers and Super Bees. What fun those cars were to drive.

Through the years I have laughed and cried. I have loved and been loved. I have felt both joy and sadness. I have smelled the fragrance of spring, saw the ocean waves pounding on the shore, and I have saw glorious sunsets melting into the night sky; as I watched the beauty of the stars in heaven appear. I have met some wonderful, kind, loving, and funny people along the way. I have laughed with them until I cried. Sadly, I have cried with them while their hearts were broken and they wept with me when my heart was broken. I truly cherish the life God so graciously gave me. My greatest regret is that it took so long for me to realize the truth: apart from Jesus Christ there is no true peace in this life and no hope for the life to come. Without knowing Jesus, a person continuously searches for the answers about life and happiness but unable to ever find it. When all is said and done, is your life going to be a success? Will you be standing in the presence of God when life ends, or will you be overcome by regret as you stand and weep in darkness?

I believe King Solomon summed life up pretty well in Ecclesiastes 12,

> Let us hear the conclusion of the whole matter: Fear God and keep His commandments, for this is man's all. For God will bring every work into judgment, including every secret thing, whether good or evil (Ecclesiastes 12:13, 14).

Final Comments: Give God a Chance

If you are struggling with alcohol or drug addiction and have tried everything to get free, but all efforts have failed—give God a chance. One of the worst things, I believe, to hinder recovery from chemical addiction was labeling drunkenness and drug addiction as a disease. Abusing drugs and alcohol is a sinful decision. Chances are no one held you down and poured alcohol down your throat, or forced pills down you. It was your foolish choice to drink alcohol and take drugs to the point of being controlled by those chemicals. Sadly, there are some forced into chemical addictions for the financial gain of others, and those who do such terrible things will be judged severally when they stand before Jesus Christ on the Day of Judgment.

Addiction is a sinful behavior which takes control of your life because of a spiritual problem. You will never resolve a spiritual problem with nonspiritual solutions. The Bible clearly describes drunkenness as a sin. How serious does God consider the sin of drunkenness? Paul warns us about the danger of alcohol abuse and how serious it is in Galatians 5 where he lists the sin of drunkenness in the same verse as murder, "Envy, murders, drunkenness, revelries, and the like; of which I tell you beforehand, just as I also told *you* in time past, that those who practice such things will not inherit the kingdom of God" (Galatians 5:21, italics theirs).

I cannot recall a Scripture that directly addresses the abuse of drugs. But anything that damages your health, your relationship with God, and destroys families is certainly sinful behavior. Alcohol and the many plants God created are to give comfort to the sick and dying—hard drink for the dying and wine for the stomach. Those provisions from God were never meant to be the focus of your life or bring harm to you or others. But mankind has an uncanny way of turning gifts from God, meant for good, into sinful consumption.

The labeling of chemical addiction as a disease gives the abuser an excuse to refuse to take responsibility for their sinful actions. A disease is something that invades your body without your permission. However, many diseases are caused by sinful decisions. (The decision to smoke cigarettes invites numerous diseases to enter your body: several types of cancer, lung disease (COPD) and heart disease to name just a few. Abusing alcohol causes liver disease and other damage to the body.)

Refusing to take responsibility for sinful actions leaves a person no hope to get free from those chains: "It's not my fault;" "I have a disease," "there's nothing I can do about it"—"I'm sick." That is a lie from the devil. God is a chain breaker and he is able to cleanse you from your sin and break the chains of addiction. Drunkenness and drug abuse are sinful choices which lead to bad behavior--disease has nothing to do with it. Give God a chance and he can begin to repair the damage those sinful behaviors have done to your soul, body, and damaged relationships.

I want you to know that I have been where you are and my heart breaks for you, because I know the freedom that awaits you if you will place your addictions in the arms of the great Physician—Jesus Christ. Do not allow yourself to be deceived any longer. Your abusive behavior is a spiritual problem. You made the choice to drink alcohol and misuse drugs, now, just as easily, you can make the choice to allow God to set you free from that awful bondage. Finding freedom from chemical addiction is a battle, but through the power of God it can be done. I am proof.

Being a child of God, gives you the power to overcome

"All things are lawful for me, but all things are not helpful. All things are lawful for me, but I will not be brought under the power of any" (1 Corinthians 6:12).

Bibliography

Blue Letter Bible. 2018. https://www.blueletterbible.org/search/ search.cfm?Criteria=things+of+this+world&t=NKJV#s=s_ primary_0_1 (accessed September 25, 2018).

Bridges, Jerry. *Trusting God Even When it Hurts.* Colorado: NavPress, 2008.

Covey, Stephen R. *The 7 Habits of Highly Effective People.* New York: Simon and Schuster, 1989.

Got Questions. *What does it mean to praise God?* 2002-2018. https:// www.gotquestions.org/praise-God.html (accessed July 07/31/18, 2018).

Graham, Billy. *Peace with God.* Garden City: Doubleday & Company, Inc., 1953.

Henry, Matthew. *Blueletter Bible.* July 14, 2018. https://www. blueletterbible.org/Comm/mhc/Mar/Mar_012.cfm (accessed July 14, 2018).

Holman Bible Dictionary. *Holman Illustrated Bible Dictionary.* Nashville: Holman Bible Publishers, 2003.

Lawrence, Brother. *The Practice of the Presence of God.* New Kensington: Whitaker House, 1982.

MacAuthor, John. *The MacAothor Bible commentary.* Nashville: Thomas Nelson, 2005.

MURASHKO, ALEX. *Views of U.S. Moral Values Slip to Seven-Year Lows.* April 10, 2014. HTTPS://WWW.CHRISTIANPOST. COM/NEWS/STATE-OF-THE-BIBLE-SURVEY-BIBLE-SKEPTICS-ON-THE-RISE-117696/.

Norman, Jim. *Views of U.S. Moral Values Slip to Seven-Year Lows.* May 22, 2017. Jim Norman https://news.gallup.com/poll/210917/views-moral-values-slip-seven-year-lows.aspx https://news.gallup.com/poll/210917/views-moral-values-slip-seven-year-lows.aspx.

The Mosby's Medical Dictionary, 9th edition. *The Free Dictionary by Farlex.* 2009. https://medical-dictionary.thefreedictionary.com/alcoholic+blackout (accessed June 9, 2018).

Tozeer, A.W. *The Root of the Righteous.* Chicago. IL.: Moody Publisher, 2015.

Printed in the United States
By Bookmasters